Gospel DNA

Five Markers of a Flourishing Church

Learning from a Movement Called "Missouri"

Michael W. Newman

Gospel DNA
Five Markers of a Flourishing Church

Ursa Publishing, San Antonio, Texas

©2016 Michael W. Newman

Printed in the United States of America

ISBN-13: 978-1532946417
ISBN-10: 1532946414

For information:
www.mnewman.org

Dedication

To the sainted Rev. Dr. Walter A. Maier
When he spoke, the world listened.
May God provide a Gospel open door like him for today.

Contents

Gospel DNA

DNA Marker One: PEOPLE

Marker One: People
Chapter One
Whitney

"For we cannot but speak of what we have seen and heard."
The Apostle Peter in Acts 4:20

Come to MY Church!

Whitney was thirteen years old when one of her friends invited her to come along with her to a Tuesday evening youth ministry gathering at church. They played some games, ate cookies, and gathered around tables in small groups to talk and pray. An adult leader asked each girl to share her "highs and lows" from the week. The little group listened to Whitney and seemed truly happy she was there. They talked about life and about Jesus' love.

The next day at school, Whitney walked through the hallways inviting people to "her church." "You have to come," she said, "Come with me to *my* church!" Just twelve hours after Whitney's first visit to church, only half a day after Whitney heard about Jesus for the very first time, she was inviting everyone to experience the same blessing. A thirteen-year-old girl from a broken home who had already been trying to find fulfillment in sexual activity and partying was now telling people they needed to hear the Gospel.

My daughter told me Whitney's story. You see, my daughter grew up in the church Whitney was invited to. I was the pastor there. I baptized my daughter at the church. As a newborn baby, my daughter was passed up and down the pew so everyone could have a turn holding her. She was part of church picnics, Vacation Bible Schools, Sunday School Christmas programs and weekly worship. She accompanied me to wedding rehearsals and waited for me while I became delayed in meetings with people.

But that day at school, Whitney stopped her in the hallway and said to her, "Abby, you have to come to MY church!"

As Abby told me the story, she smiled in amazement. This was *Whitney*. It was *her* church. A young girl far from God had become an evangelist.

What happened? It doesn't take long to notice the parallels to the stories of people throughout the ages whose lives have been transformed by the love of Jesus. Through eager disciples, God's living Word did its transforming work. Through compassionate followers of Christ, Whitney received a sense of acceptance and care she had never experienced before. The Spirit of God embraced her with friendship, hope, forgiveness, and affirmation. Whitney encountered the goodness of God and she really, really liked it. So, she began to speak about what she had seen and heard.

Whitney wanted to make sure the people around her did not miss out on this. It was too important not to share. She abandoned the usual self-consciousness of a thirteen-year-old and took the risk of roaming through the hallways of her junior high school issuing invitations to come and see what she experienced. She knew that this good thing could not be kept to herself. It had to be shared with everyone. The love that changed her life was so good, she wanted everyone to receive it. And where better to connect with people than the place she spent the majority of her day?

Led by the Holy Spirit, Whitney exhibited the DNA of Gospel movements and church multiplication. She became a microcosm of God's Kingdom movements seen across history. She was the baseline, cellular level of the development of the body of Christ. Whitney cared about people. She had a joyful zeal about multiplying her own experience of faith. She shared a specific message—one she trusted in completely. She figured out how to do that in her own context. And she sacrificed her own self-consciousness, reputation, and energy. These five characteristics stand out as five markers of what I'm calling Gospel DNA. They are:

People
Multiplication
Truth
Adaptability
Self-sacrifice

From Whitney to current church planting movements around the world, to movements that have taken place in history, it is these five characteristics that appeared over and over again as I researched the growth of God's Church. These strands form the DNA of Gospel movements.

Why a Gospel Movement?

But why should we care about the movement of the Gospel? We care for the same reason Whitney cared. We were lost and now are found. Jesus has become our refuge, strength, and salvation. We want everyone to receive this precious gift.

But as we share God's desire to see all people saved, we must also guard ourselves against our own corrupt motives. Serving God can easily become about us. We may crave fame or recognition. We may pursue a movement of the Gospel because we want to be viewed as the authority. Deep inside of each of us there is a flawed and egocentric desire to do exactly what Adam and Eve attempted in the Garden of Eden: they tried to be like God. I confess that my motives for God's mission aren't always upright and God-glorifying. Sometimes they're self-glorifying. But whenever my twisted ego-driven intentions try to take hold, I take comfort in the fact that God wants a movement of the Gospel more than anyone else. And His motives are pure, powerful, and beautiful.

Jesus said in John chapter 3, "For God so loved the world, that he gave his only Son, that whoever believes in him should not perish but have eternal life" (John 3:16). In chapter 6, Jesus commented: "For I have come down from heaven, not to do my own will but the will of him who sent me. And this is the will of him who sent me, that I should lose nothing of all that he has given me, but raise it up on the last day. For this is the will of my Father, that everyone who looks on the Son and believes in him should have eternal life, and I will raise him up on the last day" (John 6:38–40). God wants His Good News of forgiveness, new life, and eternal salvation through faith in Jesus Christ to reach the world. He wants it more than any of us.

And God graciously puts that desire into our hearts. Jeremiah said, "If I say, 'I will not mention him, or speak any more in his name,' there is in my heart as it were a burning fire shut up in my bones, and I am weary with holding it in, and I cannot" (Jeremiah 20:9). Can you relate to Jeremiah? Do you have that burning zeal to let people know about Jesus? Do you want them to know the refuge and strength you know? Do you have a deep desire to make sure the people in your life experience the friendship and restoration of the Son of God? Do you want to be certain that the people you care about receive the eternal hope Jesus has given you? I do. I know what it is like to be helpless in fear, weakness and pain. And I know the rescue and relief of the risen Christ.

I also know that eighty-percent of the people where I live do not feel it is important to be part of a church and do not consider faith to be an important part of their lives. The most rapidly growing segment of society in the United States is the one unaffiliated with any church.[1] The Christian faith is fading in importance to the new generation. And this drift from Jesus Christ has eternal consequences for millions of people.

That's why I pray for and dream of a Gospel movement in the United States. What does a Gospel movement look like? We need look no further than the global south to catch a glimpse. In the year 2000, Ying and Grace Kai pondered how they might share Christ in a region of Asia populated with over twenty million people. After starting simple training to help farmers and villagers share their faith and encourage new believers to do the same, a movement of the Gospel began to take hold. In just a decade, more

---

[1] "America's Changing Religious Landscape,"
http://www.pewforum.org/2015/05/12/americas-changing-religious-landscape/.

than 1.7 million people were baptized and more than 140,000 new house churches and small groups started in villages and cities throughout the region. This has been called the fastest-growing Church Planting Movement in the world today.[2]

In Africa, the Ethiopian Evangelical Church Mekane Yesus grew from 20,000 baptized members in 1959 to 7.8 million baptized members in 2015.[3] The exponential growth continues as this, the third largest Lutheran church body in the world, looks to outgrow The Church of Sweden and the Evangelical Lutheran Church in Tanzania to become the largest Lutheran Church in the world.

These statistics are much more than merely numbers. The numbers represent people who are receiving the gift of the forgiveness of sins and the blessing of eternal life through faith in Jesus Christ. This is happening throughout Asia, Africa and South America. While the western world becomes more secular, atheistic and apathetic, the global south is exploding with a multiplying movement of the Gospel.

I wonder if it can happen again in the west. Yes, I said "again." You see, it's happened before.

Can It Happen Here and Now?

In my work as a mission strategist, I began to study Gospel movements around the world. I noticed something compelling about the rapid church multiplication happening in the global south. The Gospel is being proclaimed by people who resemble Whitney: ordinary new believers who have been captivated by God's grace in Jesus. In reading about some of the characteristics of current Gospel movements, I began to recall some of the history of my own church denomination in the United States. I wondered if the church I'm a part of is a result of early Gospel movements in

---

[2] Smith, Steve, "Discipleship Revolution: Training for Trainers Process," Mission *Frontiers*, January-February 2011, 12.

[3] Berhanu Ofgaa, "The Lay Mission Movement in the Ethiopian Evangelical Church Mekane Yesus." Presented at the LCMS Six-Pack Conference, Dallas, Texas, March 16, 2016.

the expanding western world. Knowing some of the background of my church, I had the suspicion that my own church's history bore similarities to Gospel movements today. Upon closer examination, I was astounded.

First, I looked at statistical growth. Then I read historical documents. Next, I found writings from before the founding of my denomination and during each era of its history. Finally, I began to hear story after story about the growth of my church. The facts were indisputable. Embedded in the history of the western church—of my church!—is the answer for the twenty-first century church. The DNA of Gospel movements and church multiplication is hard-wired into who we are.

What if we could reconnect with that treasure? What if we could reinvigorate that reality?

In this book, I'll be using a small and humble denomination as a case study—my denomination: The Lutheran Church–Missouri Synod. Its development in the 1800s and 1900s reveals strands of DNA that have consistently given birth to Gospel movements throughout history. While a number of fine histories of the Missouri Synod exist, it is my hope that the analysis in this book can highlight important components of LCMS history that can easily be overlooked.

As I write, I'll be using some terms interchangeably to express the rapid multiplication of the church. My term, "Gospel movement," refers to the overall multiplication of followers of Jesus who come to faith, share their faith, make more disciples, form churches and multiply all of the above. I also use the terms "church planting," "church multiplication," and "mission movement" to convey the same phenomenon. Because "church planting" could communicate a specific methodology, I want to be sure every reader understands that when people come to faith in Jesus, they gather together as the church. A movement of the Gospel always results in local churches being born for the purpose of accomplishing God's gracious and beautiful mission.

As we consider God's movement of the Gospel, we must ask humbling and soul-searching questions: Can we acknowledge our desperation for God's grace and renounce our illusion of achievement as God's star players? Will we accept that God will move into unsavory places among unwanted people in the midst of messy and controversial life-journeys—and that He will use those very people to advance His Good News in the world? Can we embrace the fact that God's movements will not necessarily take place under the lights of fame and notoriety, but will very often happen in quiet corners and in personal relationships? Can we willingly accept that movements are led by broken people, desperate people, people of the cross of Jesus Christ, receiving His grace for each moment and sharing in His sufferings? Will we sacrifice our sinful ambition to *be* the Savior and let God be the One who leads the way and receives all glory as He moves His Kingdom forward?

That's why the title of this book is "Gospel DNA." DNA is a gift. It is not the result of our might or power. It is not found in us because of our planning or strategy. It is given to us. Gospel DNA is from the Spirit of God. DNA is not about principles, steps or programs. It is hard-wired, part of the package, formed at conception. But its markers can be detected, and by their detection you can tell who you are, where you come from, and what you're made of. Your characteristics carried by your DNA can help you understand yourself. Likewise, the characteristics of the church carried by its DNA may help you rediscover the purpose of the church and the direction you are meant to go as a follower of Jesus Christ.

So, where does Gospel DNA begin? Exactly where Whitney started: With a passionate and urgent love for people. This is the first marker of every Gospel movement. It may also be one of the most monumental challenges the church in the west faces today.

Questions for Discussion – Chapter One

1. What stood out to you in this chapter?

2. Read Acts 2:36-47. What might a movement of the Gospel look like in your community and context?

3. What challenges exist—both in you and in your broader circumstances—that might stand in the way of a Gospel movement?

4. Reflect on the five markers of Gospel DNA mentioned in this chapter: People, Multiplication, Truth, Adaptability, and Self-sacrifice. What thoughts come to your mind about how each of those characteristics can be lived out in your life and in your church?

5. Why might showing love and care for people be one of the greatest challenges for us today?

Gospel DNA Journal:

How God is leading me to new thoughts about the purpose of His church...

Where I see Gospel DNA...

Love Lost and Found

"For Christ's love compels us, because we are convinced that one died for all, and therefore all died. And he died for all, that those who live should no longer live for themselves but for him who died for them and was raised again. So from now on we regard no one from a worldly point of view."
The Apostle Paul in 2 Corinthians 5:14–16 (NIV)

Love Grown Cold

"A divine passion for souls." That phrase gripped me as I pored over the historical documents of my little denomination. From the mid-1800s through the 1950s, the expression of an intense love and care for people's eternal welfare permeated books, documents, convention resolutions and stories. This love manifested itself in innovative evangelistic efforts, in the sending of missionaries to urban areas, rural outposts and to nations around the world, and in the development of ministries that served the poor, outcast and weak. A strong and sincere love for people fueled new ministry methods, transcended boundaries, and produced a tenacious adherence to the truth of God's Word.

This love was not perfect. It was influenced by the times and shaped by circumstances and context. But it was real. Its motivation was the same as it has been for Christ's Church throughout the ages: "We love because [God] first loved us" (1 John 4:19).

I wonder if the decline of the western church in the twenty-first century is caused not by the changing culture, a shorter attention span, the dominance of the media, the rise of materialism or the drumbeat narrative of secular humanism. I wonder if the decline is caused by our diminishing love for people.

These days, loving people is not such an easy pursuit. In a busy and overstressed nation, caring about people doesn't come easy. We tend to avoid interaction with people. We pay at the pump, go to the drive-through, shop online, and press our garage door openers so we can get into the house and avoid time-consuming conversations. People are reduced to interruptions or political statements or social causes. People become burdens to our overtaxed and complicated lives. We pack our lives with things to do and end up with no room for relationships, no time for walking the journey of life with someone new—or even someone we've known for a long time.

I'm one of the culprits of this relationship unavailability and aversion. My life is very task oriented. I don't have a lot of margin for the unexpected detours people bring. I remember having twenty minutes to wash my car. When my neighbor came out to talk with me, I kept my head down and continued to labor at the task. If I stopped, I knew the car wouldn't get washed that day. The task became more important than my neighbor. I didn't ask myself how stopping might help forge a relationship. I didn't pause to consider the condition of my neighbor's soul. I just kept washing the car.

Will God one day in heaven commend me for cleaning my car? Will He recall with fondness the way I put a piece of machinery above a human being? No. That won't happen. My own heart bears evidence of a sinful tendency to put people below tasks, things, preferences and ego. But far beyond ignoring people, the body of Christ can also be exclusionary, mean and hateful. The Apostle Peter needed a vision from God to finally realize "that God shows no partiality, but in every nation anyone who fears him and does what is right is acceptable to him" (Acts 10:34–35). As believers, we need to heed Jesus' words as He spoke about the last days: "At that time many will turn away from the faith and will betray and hate each other...Because of the increase of wickedness, the love of most will grow cold" (Matthew 24:10, 12 NIV). Sometimes our hatred and coldness of love is loud and overt: We argue, criticize, discriminate and threaten. At other times it is quiet, but deadly: We patronize, enable, retreat and become distracted.

To be completely honest, there are people we—the followers of Jesus—don't really want to bring the Gospel to in a personal relationship. We hope *someone* does, but it's not our thing. And that forces us to face a very real and convicting question: Do we really love people or are we simply bothered by them? Maybe that's what our culture sees when it assesses the church these days. Studies like the book *unChristian: What a New Generation Really Thinks about Christianity...and Why It Matters* by David Kinnaman and Gabe Lyons show that younger generations in the United States have negative perceptions of the institutional church and are distancing themselves from organized religion. The inward focus of the church is palpable to them. The authors note that young people today "worry that the message [of the church] has become one of self-preservation rather than one of world restoration."[4] Even worse, the top three words and phrases used by unchurched 18-30 year olds to describe the church are: antihomosexual, judgmental, and hypocritical.[5]

All of this makes me wonder if instead of asking how we as followers of Christ can be more effective, we need to ask, "Are we passionate about bringing the beautiful message of God's grace through faith in Jesus to people or would we rather not bother with that?"

You may remember the time a Pharisee invited Jesus to dinner and a woman who lived a sinful life entered the house and began to wash Jesus' feet with her tears and expensive perfume. The Pharisee's thoughts immediately went to judgment and condemnation. His critical spirit snidely said silently about Jesus and the woman, "If this man were a prophet, he would have known who and what sort of woman this is who is touching him, for she is a sinner" (Luke 7:39). With the stroke of a master teacher, Jesus

---

[4] David Kinnaman and Gabe Lyons, *unChristian: What a New Generation Really Thinks About Christianity...and Why It Matters*, (Grand Rapids: Baker Books, 2012), 35.
[5] Kinnaman and Lyons, *unChristian*, 27.

turned to Simon the Pharisee and drove home a point that echoes into our souls today:

> "Simon, I have something to say to you."
> And he answered, "Say it, Teacher."
> "A certain moneylender had two debtors. One owed five hundred denarii, and the other fifty. When they could not pay, he cancelled the debt of both. Now which of them will love him more?"
> Simon answered, "The one, I suppose, for whom he cancelled the larger debt."
> And he said to him, "You have judged rightly."
> Then turning toward the woman he said to Simon, "Do you see this woman? I entered your house; you gave me no water for my feet, but she has wet my feet with her tears and wiped them with her hair. You gave me no kiss, but from the time I came in she has not ceased to kiss my feet. You did not anoint my head with oil, but she has anointed my feet with ointment. Therefore I tell you, her sins, which are many, are forgiven—for she loved much. **But he who is forgiven little, loves little**."
> And he said to her, "Your sins are forgiven" (Luke 7:40–48, emphasis added).

Could our lack of love signal a self-righteous rejection of the One who came to redeem us? Remember what the Apostle John said, "By this it is evident who are the children of God, and who are the children of the devil: whoever does not practice righteousness is not of God, nor is the one who does not love his brother" (1 John 3:10), and, "Anyone who does not love does not know God, because God is love" (1 John 4:8).

As people who confess the name of Jesus, we may need to stop asking, "How can we grow the church?" and start asking, "How can we begin to love people as God loved us?" Once again, the Apostle John charts the course:

Beloved, let us love one another, for love is from God, and whoever loves has been born of God and knows God. Anyone who does not love does not know God, because God is love. In this the love of God was made manifest among us, that God sent his only Son into the world, so that we might live through him. **In this is love, not that we have loved God but that he loved us and sent his Son to be the propitiation for our sins. Beloved, if God so loved us, we also ought to love one another** (1 John 4:7–11, emphasis added).

True Love

How can a church learn to love again?

The first-century church in Ephesus found itself in the same predicament: it was busy, hard-working and intolerant of falsehood. But it was loveless. Jesus spoke to that church and said, "But I have this against you, that you have abandoned the love you had at first. Remember therefore from where you have fallen; repent, and do the works you did at first" (Revelation 2:4–5).

As a church, we can think we have it all together. After all, we have the truth. We work with eternal things. We are stewards of the mysteries of God. But we can fall into the trap of thinking we have it all right all the time. We forget that we, too, are sinners. We, too, have blind spots. We, too, need to examine ourselves constantly and repent. John said, "If we say we have no sin, we deceive ourselves, and the truth is not in us" (1 John 1:8). That's a frightening statement for a church that becomes self-righteous. If we think we are right about everything and can dish out condemnation with arrogant authority, we are deceiving ourselves and have lost the truth. Paul said it very clearly, "If I speak in the tongues of men and of angels, but have not love, I am a noisy gong or a clanging cymbal. And if I have prophetic powers, and understand all mysteries and all knowledge, and if I have all faith, so as to remove mountains, but have not love, I am nothing. If I give away all I have, and if I deliver up my body to be burned, but have not love, I gain nothing" (1 Corinthians 13:1–3). Without love, all the efforts of the church are nothing.

In Jesus' parable of the Good Samaritan, the church leaders who passed by the man left for dead were doing the "right" thing. They were staying obedient to the law and not touching a dead body. But their actions were wrong. They were being loveless to their neighbor. The Samaritan did the "wrong" thing. He violated the law by coming into contact with what was considered unclean. Yet, he was right and was commended as a true neighbor because he showed love to the wounded man (Luke 10:25-37). We can think we are so right when, in actuality, we are very wrong.

Perhaps that is why the great reformer of the church, Martin Luther, began his Ninety-five Theses with the statement: "When our Lord and Master Jesus Christ said, 'Repent' (Mt 4:17), he willed the entire life of believers to be one of repentance."[6] The posture of a church that loves others is repentance.

What is repentance? First, it is a gift of God. We don't conjure up true repentance. When the believers in Jerusalem heard Peter's account of how Gentiles in Cornelius' house came to faith, we hear that "they glorified God, saying, 'Then to the Gentiles also God has granted repentance that leads to life'" (Acts 11:18). God grants repentance.

Second, simply defined, "Repentance is nothing else than to have contrition and sorrow, or terror about sin, and yet at the same time to believe in the gospel and absolution that sin is forgiven and grace is obtained through Christ."[7] A life of repentance means a life of humility and self-examination. It is a Spirit-given awareness of our flawed and sinful lives—our hesitance to share the hope we have in Jesus, our fear of other people, our sense of superiority over others, our need to exert control, our distraction from God's mission. Repentance shows itself in a life of gratitude, having received the greatest gift of all. It

---

[6] "The Ninety-Five Theses," http://www.luther.de/en/95thesen.html.

[7] Robert Kolb and Timothy J. Wengert, eds., *The Book of Concord* (Minneapolis: Fortress Press, Minneapolis, 2000), 44.

means being in awe before the Holy God who "made him to be sin who knew no sin, so that in him we might become the righteousness of God" (2 Corinthians 5:21). It is a grace-filled life, rejoicing in the fact that the Friend of Sinners has befriended us also.

A true spirit of repentance is where love begins. Sitting at the feet of Jesus to listen to His Word is how love grows.

It's no mystery why Jesus' parable of the Good Samaritan is followed by Jesus' visit to the home of Mary and Martha. Being a merciful neighbor is directly connected with the "one thing needed" (Luke 10:42). Martha was busy and distracted with many things. Mary sat at Jesus' feet, listening to what He said (Luke 10:38-42). In order to be followers of Christ who love as we have been loved, it is essential that we have a relentless focus on Jesus and resolute dedication to listening to His Word. This, of course, is not for the sole purpose of gaining knowledge, but to be "doers of the word, not hearers only" (James 1:22). Repentance always bears fruit (Luke 3:8) and the Word of God never returns empty or ineffective (Isaiah 55:11).

Just as the church in Ephesus experienced, the world, our own sinful flesh and the work of the devil always pull us away from God's Word. We may know the letter of the Word, but we drift from the Spirit of the Word. The people of Israel fell into this trap time and time again. They were condemned for living loveless lives. They went through the motions of what God required, but their sacrifices and worship became a stench to Him (see Isaiah 58 for an example). The prophet Micah voiced both the tension and calling the church experiences today:

With what shall I come before the Lord, and bow myself before God on high? Shall I come before him with burnt offerings, with calves a year old? Will the Lord be pleased with thousands of rams, with ten thousands of rivers of oil? Shall I give my firstborn for my transgression, the fruit of my body for the sin of my soul? He has told you, O man, what is good; and what does the Lord require of you but to do justice, and to love kindness, and to walk humbly with your God?" (Micah 6:6–8)

Followers of Christ who maintain a posture of repentance and who sit at the feet of Jesus to hear Him and follow Him will be led in the way of Christ's love. This was a central prayer of Paul for the church. Decades before Jesus spoke to the church in Ephesus in the book of Revelation, Paul prayed for the Ephesian Christians. He said:

I bow my knees before the Father, from whom every family in heaven and on earth is named, that according to the riches of his glory he may grant you to be strengthened with power through his Spirit in your inner being, so that Christ may dwell in your hearts through faith—that you, being rooted and grounded in love, may have strength to comprehend with all the saints what is the breadth and length and height and depth, and to know the love of Christ that surpasses knowledge, that you may be filled with all the fullness of God (Ephesians 3:14–19).

This is a prayer for the church today. The Apostle Paul knew that being a church filled with Christ's love would be the greatest challenge Christians would face. I believe it continues to be the most daunting obstacle to a movement of the Gospel in the United States today. Will we repent, hear the Word of Christ, and follow Him? Will we be filled with all the fullness of God so we can truly love people?

I didn't realize it when I began to research my denominational history, but these questions were what propelled my church body into the first of two church multiplication movements, growing from a small band of immigrants and a handful of congregations to thousands of congregations consisting of more than one million people by the early 1900s. Examining the miracle of that overflowing love in action may help us reconnect with Gospel DNA.

Questions for Discussion – Chapter Two

1. What new thoughts, insights and feelings did this chapter stir up in your mind and heart?

2. What makes your love for people grow cold?

3. How is a diminishing love for people connected with becoming more distant from Jesus? Discuss the dangers and remedies to this subtle and dangerous drift.

4. Who has shown you God's amazing love in your life? With whom do you get to share God's love these days?

5. Read Psalm 23. What are some ways love and care for people are restored in your life by your Good Shepherd?

Gospel DNA Journal:

How I am being stirred to repentance…

Who in my life needs to receive Christ's love…

Chapter Three
Love Grows

"It is too small a thing for you to be my servant to restore the tribes of Jacob and bring back those of Israel I have kept. I will also make you a light for the Gentiles, that you may bring my salvation to the ends of the earth."
God speaking in Isaiah 49:6 (NIV)

The Stage is Set

Carl Walther was just twenty-seven years old when he stepped aboard the Johann Georg, a ship bound from the port city of Bremerhaven to the United States of America. It was a bold step to start a new life. He traveled with a group of nearly seven-hundred disenchanted citizens of the Kingdom of Saxony. It was autumn in 1838. What is now modern-day Germany was, at that time, a confederation of loosely connected state monarchies. Many citizens of Saxony and the surrounding states were dissatisfied with government corruption and oppression. The local unrest would culminate in the revolutions of 1848 and the unification of Germany. Walther and his band of Saxons were frustrated because of religious oppression. After the Prussian Union of 1817, their Lutheran Church was forced to sacrifice its distinctive teachings and beliefs in order to unite with the Reformed Church.

The Saxons were also loyal followers of Pastor Martin Stephan. He convinced the group that it was time to leave Saxony for the United States so they could exercise their religious prerogatives freely. But Martin Stephan had a secret. While gaining a strong following as an effective pastor and teacher as well as a staunch defender of Lutheran doctrine, self-interest was harbored in Stephan's heart. People whispered about his evening walks with young women. Just one month before his departure for the United States, a servant girl charged Stephan with improper conduct. His congregation followed with formal complaints of an immoral life, the frequent neglect of pastoral duties, and embezzlement.[8] Stephan's followers defended him and were able to extricate him from the legal proceedings in Saxony. But just six months after the group's arrival in the United States, Stephan's facade crumbled.

By May of 1839 Stephan became careless with people he had enlisted as leaders. His arrogance and recklessness swelled as he ignored advice and critiques. Before the ships arrived in New Orleans for the trek up the Mississippi River to Perry County and St. Louis, Missouri, Stephan had declared himself Bishop over the band of immigrants. He used the community treasury liberally, buying expensive furnishings for himself and making certain he was comfortable—even as the rank and file struggled. Then women began to come forward. Some recounted Stephan's attempts to seduce them. Others confessed adulterous relationships with him. The pastors who heard this news were shocked. Behind their quest for religious freedom was the abuse of power, the infliction of pain and shame, and consistent deception. The man who claimed to be a spiritual leader was concealing dark and corrupt ulterior motives.

The young pastor, Carl Walther, was crushed and disillusioned. The community was shocked and demoralized. But action had to be taken. To Walther's dismay, the Saxon leaders chose him to confront Martin Stephan. After withering in the presence of his mentor and failing in his attempts at personal confrontation, Walther finally invited the residents of the Perry County colony to join him for a worship service on Sunday. After the worship service was over, Walther announced the indiscretions of Stephan to the crowd.[9] Days later, Stephan was removed from office and sent away from the Saxon settlement. He boarded a boat

---

[8] Walter O. Forster, *Zion on the Mississippi* (St. Louis: Concordia Publishing House, 1953), 183.
[9] Forster, *Zion*, 390-410.

that crossed the Mississippi river to Illinois and spent the remainder of his life there.

Gospel DNA Takes Hold

This twisted and tragic odyssey affected Walther very deeply and changed the course of Lutheranism in America. What started out as an exclusive and inwardly thinking transition to the new world, became a wake-up call to the true nature and purpose of the church. Walther felt tremendous guilt about his part in the Saxon immigration debacle. His conscience was stirred to repentance. In November of 1839, a day of penance was observed as the group of immigrants pondered their next steps. It was the beginning of a new approach to being the church—albeit a rough and uncertain beginning. This pattern of observing a day of repentance carried through into Walther's ministry for years to come. Thirty-one years after that first day of repentance, Walther referenced his congregation's annual day of penitence as he preached the sermon, "We Are No Longer What We Were!" at his church in St. Louis. In the sermon he emphasized the congregation's need to repent regarding its faith in God and love for neighbor. Walther looked back to the beginning of the congregation as he commented, "What zeal there was to bring also others to God's Word, and what joy if only one soul was won, even though it were a poor wood cutter!" He went on to issue the convicting question: "Has not the zeal to win souls practically died out among us?" Repentance and a renewed approach to the Gospel would wrest the church from the dangerous clutches of apathy, lovelessness, and lack of concern for people's eternal welfare.[10]

This is what happened in the fall of 1839. With a spirit of repentance Walther was drawn back to the Scriptures and Martin Luther's writings. He was deeply troubled, but God was changing him. One year after the disaster with Stephan, Walther wrote to his older brother and confessed:

---

[10] Henry J. Eggold, trans., *Selected Writings of C.F.W. Walther: Selected Sermons*, Ed., August R. Suelflow, (St. Louis: Concordia Publishing House, 1981), 157, 159.

Thereupon follow the shameful idolatry with Stephan, the sectarian exclusiveness, the condemnation of other upright people, the departure from many essentials of the Lutheran Church, and who will name it all? Every sad look of a member from our congregations is to me like an accuser before God; my conscience blames me for all the broken marriages which occurred among us; it calls me a kidnapper, a robber of the wealthy among us, a murderer of those who lie buried in the sea and the many who were stricken down here…[11]

Walther was heartbroken by his blindness, his gullibility, and his selfishness. Families were torn apart when the Saxons fled to the United States. Nearly sixty immigrants died at sea when the ship Amalia was lost and never made it to port. People lost their financial resources, their health and their lives. For all of it, Walther felt the weight of personal guilt. As his nagging sense of remorse and unfaithfulness grew, and as the Saxon laypeople insisted on having a part in the leadership and decision-making of the church, Walther's view of the church changed. Moving from inward and exclusionary thinking, Walther became a champion of connecting with other believers and reaching people who did not know the Good News of Salvation in Jesus.

In an 1845 letter to William Sihler, a missionary leader in Ohio who became the first president of the Lutheran Seminary in Fort Wayne, Indiana, Walther said:

We, who in unbelievable blindness formerly permitted ourselves to be led by Stephan, have special reason to seek out those of orthodox faith…God knows that we ourselves under Stephan had nothing else in mind but to prove ourselves completely faithful to the true Lutheran Church. But there was nothing which caused us to fail in this very thing more than our stubborn exclusiveness.[12]

---

[11] Forster, *Zion*, 515.

[12] Roy A. Suelflow, trans., ed., *Selected Writings of C.F.W. Walther: Selected Letters*, (St. Louis: Concordia Publishing House, 1981), 86.

Carl Walther, known as C.F.W. Walther in Lutheran history, never forgot the costly lessons learned as a disciple of Martin Stephan. Walther pursued truth without love. He practiced faith without deeds that served his neighbor. He chased a cause without regard for people. But that changed. People—a love for the people for whom Christ died—became a central focus and passion for Walther.

Some scholars are not convinced about Walther's heart for outreach and desire for mission. A great deal of Walther's writings were focused on the defense of pure doctrine and the proof that the Missouri Synod was truly the church. Walther became, in the eyes of many—and very rightly—the father of confessional Lutheranism in the United States. His zeal for the purpose of the Gospel, however, the heart of pure teaching, cannot be overlooked.

In a stirring 1842 sermon entitled, "Bringing Souls to Christ: Every Christian's Desire and Duty," Walther proclaimed:

The Christian looks upon his neighbor with sadness when he knows that the neighbor does not yet know the Gospel…

A Christian might even wish that he could persuade the whole world to know that they can leave their sins and futile life behind and take hold of Christ. The holy desire to bring souls to Christ begins immediately, as soon as the light of true faith comes into a person's soul bringing with it the fire of true love for others. This holy desire is inseparable from a true faith. Whoever has no desire to bring someone else to the knowledge of the saving Gospel has certainly not yet come to know the heavenly power himself.

Dear friends, through faith a Christian receives not only the holy desire to bring souls to Christ. He receives this task as a sacred duty. No one should say, "I am not a pastor, teacher, or a preacher; let them teach, instruct, comfort, and lead souls to Christ. I wish to remain in my own vocation." No. Christian, you are baptized, and through holy baptism you have already been called and anointed to be a priest of God.

Go through all the chief parts of the Catechism and in each part you will find the declaration that a Christian should care for the salvation of his neighbor.

The Christian Church is a great mission-house. Each Christian in it is a missionary sent out by God into his own circle to convert others to Christ.[13]

With a burning zeal for the Gospel, Walther became passionate about people. He wanted to join with people who confessed the truth of God's Saving Word and he wanted to reach as many people as possible who had not yet received the gifts of forgiveness and eternal life in Jesus Christ. This newfound passion, this Holy-Spirit-ignited desire, would set into motion one of the great Gospel movements of the nineteenth and twentieth centuries. It would solidify the DNA of what developed into the Lutheran Church–Missouri Synod. It would help begin one of the most dynamic church planting movements of the 1800s and 1900s.

Walther's love and care for people, his deep passion for their eternal welfare, did not fade as he became established as the leader of the Lutheran Church–Missouri Synod. He served as president of the denomination, as a professor at the St. Louis seminary, and as pastor of a multi-site church in St. Louis. As the years passed, his emphasis on forming relationships with people so they could know their Savior did not wane. In an article written in 1862, Walther emphasized that God's precious Word of salvation was not to be hidden or restricted. In the article, he commented on the purpose of the eternal Gospel delivered by the angel in Revelation 14:6-7. Going back to Martin Luther's day, Walther said that this Gospel "was not the temporal, transitory message of vain human doctrine that Luther proclaimed, but an *eternal* Gospel,

---

[13] C.F.W. Walther, "Bringing Souls to Christ: Every Christian's Desire and Duty," Bruce Cameron, trans., *Missio Apostolica* (May 1998): 6-16.

the pure, clear, unalterable, and imperishable Word of the Most High. [Luther's] calling was not to give this bread of life to the little parish in Wittenberg, but *'to every nation and tribe and tongue and people.'*"[14]

Later in 1872, Walther compiled his Pastoral Theology book drawn from articles he wrote over a period of six years from 1865 through 1871. The articles gave practical advice to pastors about how to conduct ministry. Walther introduced the book by telling pastors that there was an ultimate purpose to all pastoral work and to all theology. He said, "Pastoral Theology is the God-given practical ability of the soul, acquired through certain auxiliary means, by virtue of which a minister of the church is enabled to carry out all his functions as such in a valid and legitimate way, to the glory of God, for the salvation of his listeners and himself...It is practical in general because its purpose, as that of all theology, consists in leading the sinner to salvation through faith."[15]

The purpose of all theology was directed toward people— people who needed to be led to salvation through faith in Jesus Christ. Throughout his life as a newcomer to the United States, Walther was consistent in his focus on the salvation of people whom God loved so much that He gave His one and only Son. This emphasis linked the spread of the Gospel from his generation and all generations past to the worldwide Gospel movements of today.

C.F.W. Walther died in 1887, but, by God's grace, his love for people and his concern for people's eternities continued to permeate the network of churches he helped start. What unfolded was a miraculous and gracious gift from God that spread farther than anyone ever imagined. I know this because Walther's love for people ended up changing my life.

---

[14] Herbert J.A. Bouman trans., *Editorials from Lehre und Wehre* (St. Louis: Concordia Publishing House, 1981), 104.

[15] C.F.W. Walther, *Walther's Pastoral Theology*, trans. John M. Drickamer (New Haven, Missouri: Lutheran News, Inc., 1995). 8-9.

Questions for Discussion – Chapter Three

1. What thoughts and insights did the story of C.F.W. Walther stir up in you?

2. The history in this chapter shows a decisive turning point. What turning point has God caused, or is God causing now, to bring you back to the Kingdom focus He desires?

3. Look back at the quotes from C.F.W. Walther. What phrases of his resonate in your life right now and what new ideas for outreach do they give you?

4. Who in your life do you love so much that you would like to persuade them "that they can leave their sins and futile life behind and take hold of Christ." Share a list—or make a list—so you can pray for and look for opportunities to share Jesus with loved ones who may not know Him.

5. Read Acts 1:6-8. What larger group of people is the Holy Spirit leading you to be concerned about in order to reach them with the Gospel?

Gospel DNA Journal:

Turning points in my life when God redirected me…

How I need to be patient with people who are struggling…

Marker One: People
Chapter Four
The Most Precious Gift

"Little children, let us not love in word or talk but in deed and in truth."
The Apostle John in 1 John 3:18

Caring About People

One hundred years after C.F.W. Walther died, I was ordained as a pastor in the denomination he helped start, the Lutheran Church–Missouri Synod (LCMS). It's a small church body with a membership consisting of less than one percent of the United States' population. It's a conservative, Bible-believing group. Perhaps hanging on to the name "Missouri" keeps us humble as we remember our not-so-glorious beginnings. But this little denomination has impacted millions of lives throughout the nation and world because of its deep and sincere love for people. One of its primary concerns has been the eternal welfare of people's souls.

God used C.F.W. Walther to help embed that DNA in the denomination. But it wasn't just him. While Walther was digging out of his disappointment and depression in St. Louis, another Lutheran missionary in the United States was trying to rally missionaries to come to his aid. In 1838, Friedrich Wyneken arrived in the United States. Indiana would be his home base as he began a ministry that would establish him, according to C.F.W. Walther, as: "A spiritual father to thousands, to whole regions of America an apostle."[16] Wyneken's passion for reaching the lost

---

[16] Robert E. Smith, "Wyneken as Missionary: Mission in the Life and Ministry of Friedrich Conrad Dietrich Wyneken," in *Let Christ Be Christ: Theology,*

sent him on horseback throughout the Midwest, baptizing, preaching, and fostering relationships with German-speaking people who were not connected with a church. The conditions were harsh and many people were in no mood to receive a preacher of the Gospel. Seeing the swelling numbers of people who were unchurched and in need of the saving message of Christ, Wyneken sent a letter to Germany pleading for more missionaries to help in this Gospel cause. His 1844 tract said:

> Where would you and I and all Christians be, had the Lord not sought *that which was lost*? Ought it not rather touch our hearts when we see before us the fearful danger of obduracy to which our brethren must eventually come if they go without the Word and the sacraments any longer? And whose fault is it? Ought not the church, as a good mother, to have set out long ago through her servants and gone after these languishing children, dying in wretchedness, in order to help them?[17]

Wyneken's love for people and passionate concern for their eternity moved Wilhelm Loehe, a pastor in Germany, to begin training and sending missionaries to the United States. No one knows the exact number, but some estimate that Loehe sent hundreds of workers to help reach both the growing population of immigrants and the indigenous Native Americans with the Good News of Jesus. Wyneken's group would partner with Walther's group to form the Lutheran Church–Missouri Synod in 1847. God used this partnership to implant the DNA of a passionate Gospel-focused love and care for people into the lifeblood of the LCMS. Over the years some scholars have attributed the mission component of the LCMS to Wyneken's influence alone. But, clearly, both Walther and Wyneken were stirred to a Spirit-given

---

Ethics and World Religions in the Two Kingdoms, ed. Daniel N. Harmelink (Huntington Beach, California.: Tentatio Press, 1999): 323.

[17] Carl Meyer, Moving *Frontiers*, (St. Louis: Concordia Publishing House, 1964), 95.

zeal for seeking the lost and rescuing the souls of God's precious people. This DNA was passed along to future generations.

My pastor, Walter Fisher, was one of the many servants of the church filled with this Gospel DNA. He graduated from Concordia Seminary, St. Louis, Missouri in 1947. In a booklet written that year called "How the Missouri Synod was Born," a chapter told Friedrich Wyneken's story. Study questions were included after the chapter. One asked, "What qualities made Wyneken a successful missionary?" My pastor jotted two answers at the bottom of the page. He noted: "True Christian fervor. Love of souls."

The DNA of a deep love and care for people in the name of Jesus was alive and well in the 1940s. This fact shows itself in the consistent refrain that appears throughout the years in many writings of my little denomination: People matter. Relationships are what count most. Jesus died for all. We have the great privilege and calling to love the people for whom Christ gave His life. We are to spare no energy in building relationships with those who have not yet received the gift of eternal life.

The grace of God for His precious people is a strong strand of DNA that never fades in the first one hundred plus years of my denomination's history. During this time, the church body started an average of one new church every week. One new church every week for one hundred years! Soul-winning was taken seriously by Christians in this movement.

In 1927, a series of small books called "Men and Missions" was produced by the Lutheran Church Missouri Synod's publishing arm, Concordia Publishing House. The fifth volume of the series was called, *The Wide-Open Island City, Home Mission Work in a Big City*, and was written by a pastor named Carl A. Giesler. In the book he tells the true story of his effort to start a new church near Detroit, Michigan. As he recounts the trials and blessings of planting a church, the DNA of valuing people shines through. With passion for people displayed openly, Giesler asked, "But when has a missionary done enough for a lost soul?"[18]

Five years later, Pastor John H.C. Fritz, wrote *Pastoral Theology*, the textbook for young seminarians as they prepared for ministry. Fritz, a pastor and mission board chairman turned professor, emphasized the need to be devoted to the holistic welfare of people. He pleaded with students:

> In the United States more than one half of the people are said to be unchurched. Toward these the Church has a twofold duty: gathering in, or Christianizing, the unchurched living in territories surrounding an established church and establishing new churches by Christianizing the unchurched in territories where there is no established orthodox church...Essentially, of course, the work must be done in the same way. Since every Christian is by virtue of his Christianity a missionary, a pastor should instruct his people that every Christian individually and personally should seek to win souls for Christ.[19]

The conversation shaped students to connect with people and fashioned the hearts of believers to value every life. In a 1943 booklet called, *The Approach to the Unchurched*, Pastor Philip Lange carried the torch to people in the pews:

> No Individual Christian can escape his responsibility to God! The service which God requires of His children in spreading His Word and bringing many souls to righteousness is a test and proof of loyalty to Him. This duty is not transferable.[20]

---

[18] Carl A. Giesler, *The Wide-Open Island City, Home Mission Work in a Big City*, Ed. L. Fuerbringer (St. Louis: Concordia Publishing House, 1927), 40.

[19] John H.C. Fritz, *Pastoral Theology*, (St. Louis: Concordia Publishing House, 1932), 285, 289.

[20] Philip Lange, The *Approach to the Unchurched*, (St. Louis: Concordia Publishing House, 1943), 10-11.

Lange emphasized to the reader, "Passion for souls is the most necessary qualification of any evangelistic endeavor." He then proceeded to root a strong love for people in the Bible and in the history of the Lutheran Church–Missouri Synod. Lange mentioned Friedrich Wyneken's passionate drive to reach the lost. He then traced the pathway of this active love for people to the original founders from Saxony, "Our Saxon pilgrim fathers, consumed with this divine passion for souls, preached, wrote, organized, and directed all their abilities and energies to promote the spreading of the Gospel for the conversion of sinners."[21]

The author summed up his desperate appeal to every Christian by bringing the reader back to Jesus, "Let us never give up a lost soul until that person is dead...No case was hopeless to Christ, the Master Soul Winner."[22] The love of Jesus Christ was the Gospel motivation to care about others.

In the 1947 centennial celebration book, *A Century of Grace*, author Walter A. Baepler urged the members of the Lutheran Church–Missouri Synod to "reconsecrate themselves to the work of the Lord." He noted that the twentieth century purpose of the denomination was to reach unchurched Americans. The statistics backed up the claim. Since 1918, 189,945 adults had confessed their new faith at the altars of Missouri Synod churches.[23] Caring about people was not just talk. Valuing people's lives and eternities was at the heartbeat of the movement called "Missouri." The numbers showed that eighteen new adult converts in the Lutheran Church–Missouri Synod confessed salvation by grace alone through faith alone in Jesus Christ every day for nearly thirty years.

But the leaders of this Gospel movement didn't want this passionate love and concern for people to fade into ingratitude, indifference, or inaction. In a book published by the General Centennial Committee of the Lutheran Church Missouri Synod,

---

[21] Lange, *The Approach*, 15-16.

[22] Lange, *The Approach*, 25.

[23] Walter Baepler, A *Century of Grace: A History of the Missouri Synod 1847-1947* (St. Louis: Concordia Publishing House, 1947), 357.

author and LCMS assistant to the president Lawrence Meyer communicated the ongoing desperate need for reaching people with the message of the Gospel—zealous action rooted in the forefathers of the church:

> When we think of the tremendous necessity of preaching the Gospel of Christ Jesus to a billion pagan peoples, to a world driven by lust and greed headlong into another world war, to a Protestantism devoid of Christ, to a slowly disintegrating Lutheranism, then the challenge of our times comes over us with such overwhelming force that only with faith and courage and a Christ-centered passion for souls such as filled our forefathers can we even begin to meet it.[24]

The author of this little but powerful book went on to emphasize personal missionary zeal in place of an institutional approach to outreach. In a powerful plea, he addressed the laypeople and pastors of the church:

> In contrast to that lion-hearted faith of the early Christians and the heroic sacrifices which it cost our forefathers to leave us the heritage which we possess today, we ask ourselves, What have we done, and what are we doing, to make Christianity a moving, living faith in the hearts and lives of men and women in the world? What have you laymen done for the Church today? What have you as laymen done to prove to the world that your faith is a moving, living faith? How many of you can claim the distinction of having been the means of winning one soul during the past year? Is that a harsh and searching question? Let me ask again, How many of you have any reason to believe that directly you have been made the means this year of the salvation of a single soul? I will go farther and ask those of you who are among the older Christians, Have you any reason to believe that ever since you have become a member of

---

[24] L. Meyer, *Torch Bearers*, (St. Louis: General Centennial Committee of the Evangelical Lutheran Synod of Missouri, Ohio, and Other States, 1937), 19.

the Church you have been the direct means of leading a soul to Christ?

This is an indictment not only against the laity but at the same time against us preachers. How often have we not preached the Word of God to you, and yet how seldom have we wept over you! How often have we failed to pray, charge, adjure you, to become winners of souls![25]

The passion for people flows from each word. The drive to care about relationships that lead to eternal life bursts from each syllable. It is DNA that cannot be denied. Even in the "post-church" and "post-Christian" era of the twenty-first century, this DNA bids us outward, outside the church walls, ever calling us to love people, connect with people, and understand that many people still need to receive the blessing of eternal life in Jesus Christ.

This DNA, firmly implanted in the Missouri Synod, changed my life. A Lutheran pastor connected with my immigrant Greek grandfather and his new French bride in Chicago, willingly performing their marriage ceremony at city hall. The same Lutheran pastor presided at the funeral of my grandfather's wife when she died much too young, still in the prime of life. A Lutheran children's home cared for two of my grandfather's children when he had to give them up during his turbulent and grief-torn life as a new single father. A Lutheran congregation embraced my grandfather's new family when he remarried and added three new children to the seven he had with his first wife. A Lutheran youth ministry called "The Walther League" provided the setting where my parents met and fell in love. Lutheran schools became the place where my brothers and I were educated and discipled in our early years. This was not an institutional progression. It was relational. Over and over throughout the years, people cared. They reached out to my family—non-German, sporadic church attenders—because they cared about us, both our eternal welfare and our current needs. People mattered. We

---

[25] L. Meyer, *Torch Bearers*, 53-54.

mattered. As a result, I was given the most precious gift I could have ever received: the gift of eternal life in Jesus Christ. And that gift still needs to be shared with so many people today. But how? This book uses a small slice of history to reconnect us to Gospel DNA. But this book is also about application and action. What are some next steps that will rekindle in our hearts love for God's precious people?

Questions for Discussion – Chapter Four

1. How did this chapter cause you to think differently about the church and your role in it?

2. "Loving souls," "winning souls," and being a "soul-winner" are terms that may be considered old-fashioned. What new expressions capture the spirit of these terms in our day and for our work as followers of Jesus?

3. In this chapter you heard from several people who speak passionately about reaching those who do not know Jesus. What do you learn from them about loving people in the name of Jesus?

4. Whom has God put in your life to reach with the eternal hope of Jesus? Think about your faith impact on family, friends, and people far away.

5. Read Acts 4:13-20. What does "true Christian fervor" mean today? What does it look like for an individual believer and for a church?

Gospel DNA Journal:

How God might use me to be a "soul-winner"...

Why am I passionate about the message of the Gospel...

Chapter Five

How to Care

"Love is patient and kind; love does not envy or boast; it is not arrogant or rude. It does not insist on its own way; it is not irritable or resentful; it does not rejoice at wrongdoing, but rejoices with the truth. Love bears all things, believes all things, hopes all things, endures all things. Love never ends."
The Apostle Paul in 1 Corinthians 13:4–8

Can We Really Show Love and Care?

Love and care for people is the DNA of the Gospel. The "Gospel in a nutshell" begins, "For God so loved the world" (John 3:16). God loves people—He loves us, all of us. He loves you. As the Apostle John said, "This is love: not that we loved God, but that he loved us and sent his Son as an atoning sacrifice for our sins" (1 John 4:10 NIV). God's love is a gift—a life-transforming, heart-renewing, eternal life-bestowing gift. How can we, then, as God's people, show this love to others? How can we look outward and care for people when our culture and our self-centered natures call us to look inward and after our interests alone? An important part of the answer is to remember what the Apostle John emphasized: "We love because God first loved us" (1 John 4:19).

God is the One who implants Gospel DNA into our lives as He reaches us here and now through His incarnational work among us. The Apostle Paul summarized this dynamic when he said, "Do you not know that all of us who have been baptized into Christ Jesus were baptized into his death? We were buried therefore with him by baptism into death, in order that, just as Christ was raised from the dead by the glory of the Father, we too might walk in newness of life" (Romans 6:3–4). Because of His grace, God comes to us in baptism and implants new DNA. His living Word takes root in our hearts as we listen. It is no longer we who live, but Christ who lives in us. We now live by faith in the Son of God who loved us and gave His life for us (Galatians 2:20).

How can we love people? How can we care about flawed, messy, complicated, inconvenient and sometimes evil people? Martin Luther King, Jr., a namesake of the initiator of the Lutheran movement, said, "We love men not because we like them, nor because their ways appeal to us, nor even because they possess some kind of divine spark. We love every man because God loves him."[26] The Apostle Paul agreed. He was once a man who hated people who were not like him—people who broke religious laws, lived in impurity, and opposed his point of view. But the love of Christ transformed his outlook and action. He said that the love of Christ now "has its way with us all," for from now on "we regard no one according to the flesh" (2 Corinthians 5:14, 16). This transformation propels us outward in love:

> Therefore, if anyone is in Christ, he is a new creation. The old has passed away; behold, the new has come. All this is from God, who through Christ reconciled us to himself and gave us the ministry of reconciliation; that is, in Christ God was reconciling the world to himself, not counting their trespasses against them, and entrusting to us the message of reconciliation. Therefore, we are ambassadors for Christ, God making his appeal through us (2 Corinthians 5:17–20).

Paul saw people through the eyes of Jesus—the One who died for all. But are we really seeing people that way? Is the body of Christ manifesting the Gospel DNA of loving and caring for people? Is your church? Over the past four or five decades, my denomination has been in decline. My church has been in what I call a "pause." Please note that many wonderful things are happening in the Missouri Synod. The Gospel is being proclaimed in vibrant ways in many places. People filled with the love of Christ are reaching out and seeing lives transformed. New people

---

[26] Philip Yancey, *Soul Survivor*, (New York: Galilee, Doubleday, 2003), 28.

are coming to faith in Jesus and being given the gifts of the forgiveness of sins and eternal life. The church, after all, is people, and I have witnessed the beauty of Gospel DNA in so many wonderful people in my own denomination. Overall, however, our church is shrinking. While some very strong congregations are growing and vibrant, a large percentage of local congregations are plateaued or declining. The number of baptisms continues to decrease. Funds to start new ministries are becoming scarce. The younger generation is leaving.

My purpose in being honest about my church's decline is not to be critical, depressing or disheartening. Understanding the facts is an important step in being led to repentance and to humbly hearing God's Word for us in this season of our existence. And that's exactly what this is: a season. My denomination has experienced "pauses" in the past. Each pause was just that, a pause and not a failure. Historically, the pauses served as recalibration and teaching times for a new culture and context. They were healing and preparing times. If we believe God has forgotten us during the pauses, we miss His faithful presence, His teaching and His preparation.

As you read this book, your church may be in a pause. What, then, does the Gospel DNA of love and care for people look like? How can your church and my church reconnect with this Spirit-embedded characteristic of His Church? If you're planting a church, how can your new faith community live out the vibrant Gospel DNA God gives?

Care About Each Other

First, God's people care about each other.

I was blessed to be part of a beautiful mission church early in my ministry. The people in that congregation demonstrated an incredible, Spirit-filled love and care. A selflessness for the sake of the Gospel was evident in virtually every person. Each veteran member shared this Gospel DNA with every new person. The people truly cared about each other. In addition to developing what they called a "Care Network," in which people helped each other with day-to-day needs, prepared meals for people going through difficult times, sent cards of prayer and care to hurting individuals far and wide, and stepped up to show Christ's love in beautiful ways, the people also knew how to handle disagreements. This is a key component of developing and stewarding the love and care of Christ in a local congregation and in the broader context of Christianity. You need to know how to confront and manage dissonance well.

Every church has disagreements. Believers have a variety of opinions. And most every church has a healthy number of people who believe that their opinions should win the day. But handling the variety of viewpoints can either be a devastating defeat or a beautiful victory for God's people. The church needs to be confronted with the fact that the world is watching how we handle conflict. If arguments, yelling, political manipulation, gossip, power plays, and meanness prevail, the church becomes a poor witness to the world. In addition, Christian people have feelings. Kindness to one another is of utmost importance. We're not here to wound each other. As Christ loves us and cares for us, we love and care for each other.

I'll never forget a man named Chuck at the mission congregation I was privileged to serve. When the congregation decided to call me as its pastor, Chuck disagreed with the decision. He voted against the proposed action. I was too young, didn't have enough experience and didn't fit the profile they originally set their sights on. The church was a declining new mission that just lost the original church planter. It needed someone with planting experience to help regain momentum. He voted "no." But he was in the minority that day and the congregation decided to invite me to consider becoming the next pastor. What did Chuck do? Did he quit? Did he yell? Did he talk behind the backs of the people who voted for me? Did he try to sabotage my ministry after I arrived? No. Chuck trusted the movement of the Holy Spirit, continued to love his fellow believers in that small body of Christ, and leaned into serving with gusto. I didn't find out about the vote until years later. Chuck stood up in a congregational meeting and reminded everyone how he voted. He wanted to let everyone know that he now saw why the Holy Spirit worked the way He did. He confessed he was wrong and thanked everyone for following the wisdom God gave them. He expressed love and care for his fellow believers.

Chuck was a tough guy. He was a man's man. But he was also a humble, repentant and self-sacrificial servant of the Lord Jesus Christ. He was a shining example of how God's people care for each other. If you want the Gospel DNA of love and care to prevail in your church, begin by humbly and self-sacrificially loving and caring for each other—especially when it's most difficult: during times of disagreement and conflict. The Apostle Paul emphasized this to the early church. He said, "Be completely humble and gentle; be patient, bearing with one another in love. Make every effort to keep the unity of the Spirit through the bond of peace" (Ephesians 4:2–3 NIV). What work needs to be done in your community of faith to grow in kindness to one another and to grow in handling disputes well? Begin by being relentless about loving each other. But don't stop there. There is much more.

Care About the Community

Second, God's people care about the community.

If you want to exit a season of "pause," you need to fight the gravitational pull of inward thinking. The church has much to do, a lot to take care of, business to handle, and schedules of activities to manage. People have needs, and church life can be extremely busy. It can be so busy that followers of Christ have no time or opportunity to show love and care to people outside their local congregation. It's ironic, isn't it? Jesus said, "Go into all the world and proclaim the gospel to the whole creation" (Mark 16:15), but, too often, the church gets too busy to venture outside its own walls!

A big part of my ministry these days is to work with missionaries. They're local missionaries who plant churches and reach out to the many people who do not know Christ right here in the United States. A common theme of these stellar servants is their approach to community leaders. They get to know school superintendents and principals, local police officers and social workers, non-profit leaders and business owners. They take time to sit down with key people in the community in order to ask them, "What do you need that would help make this community better?" Then they listen and learn. They let the Holy Spirit lead them to respond effectively for their unique context. They encourage people of the church to do the same, discovering where God might be opening doors for them to share His love and care.

Please know that I am not advocating throwing away the proclamation of the Gospel for a weak and watered-down social Gospel. Not at all. I am talking about how the church shows Christ's love and care to the community. I am encouraging the church to be part of the fabric of the community so the beautiful Gospel of Jesus Christ can have hands, feet, and a platform for proclamation. This is not about using people to sneak in the Gospel. It's about shining the light of Christ's love into darkness so people can truly know Him.

I know of a local congregation that is embracing an immigrant and refugee population in its neighborhood. The people of the congregation are developing real friendships with these newcomers to the United States. They are eating together, helping some refugees learn how to drive, and talking about spiritual things. These new neighbors—many who do not know Christ—are getting to know Him through word and deed.

If you want to see the Gospel DNA of love and care flourish, filling the church with new and vibrant life, do something to care about your community. Make genuine room in your life for the people around you and share the fullness of Christ's love and gifts.

Care About People in Your Life

Third, as one redeemed by Jesus, you care about people in your life.

Too often, when followers of Jesus hear about reaching out to other people with the Good News, they immediately think of scary and unfamiliar situations. Does God want them to sell everything they have and move to a foreign country? Should they begin to knock on doors in unfamiliar neighborhoods? Do they need to confront people who are hostile to religion?

But God's mission doesn't begin far away. It begins at home among the people God has placed in your life. If you devote your time and energy to everyone but the people you know and love the most, you're missing out on being a Gospel influence in the very place you can be most effective. There is no more thorough Gospel-sharing and discipleship that take place than that of a parent with a child or a husband and wife with each other. Family members, friends, co-workers and people you spend most of your life with are people you need to care about.

In his book, *Surprising Insights from the Unchurched*, Thom Rainer notes how important family relationships are. Marion came to faith in Jesus at age seventy. She was an unchurched unbeliever until she heard the Gospel message at an Easter presentation in a local church. How did she get there? Marion said, "My niece invited me." After pausing for a moment she said, "No one ever invited me to church before. Why is that?" Rainer's research showed that the most influential people in connecting the unchurched to faith in Jesus are family members. Forty-two percent of formerly unchurched people listed family members as the ones who influenced them most to come to church.[27] As a follower of Christ, you are called to show the love and care of Jesus to family members. It's not always easy and, sometimes, it's very nerve-racking. But if every believer started with his or her own built-in mission field of loved ones, the Gospel would go far and the church would continue to grow.

Care About the World

Fourth, God's people care about the world.

While this can refer to international outreach and the importance of sharing the Gospel in nations around the globe, I

---

[27] Thom S. Rainer, *Surprising Insights from the Unchurched* (Grand Rapids: Zondervan, 2001), 81-82.

want to emphasize another aspect of a Christian's love and care for the world. As God's people, we need to learn to truly love and care about all the people around us—people who are *in* the world and *of* the world at this time in their lives. A significant percentage of people in our own communities are not following Christ and aren't even thinking about Him.

This reality presents questions about which we as Christ's Church must enter into thoughtful, meaningful and civil dialog:

- How can God's family exhibit authentic care and show His life-transforming love to all people—including people who are cast aside and marginalized by our culture?
- How can we develop a vocabulary that doesn't demean people who are not following Christ? If we continue to label people in negative ways as unbelievers, sinners and outsiders, are we communicating respect and love to all the people for whom Jesus died?
- How can we promote ways to be in authentic and mutual relationships with people who are not aligned with Biblical values and teaching without being afraid of forsaking our faith or being labeled as other than orthodox?
- How can we build bridges to people and communities that are diametrically opposed to our Biblical confession and values?

If local congregations, regional networks and national denominations can enter into dialog and begin to develop answers to these questions, the church will be able to take significant steps in bringing the precious gift of life in Jesus to the world.

Gospel DNA: People

True love, concern, and time for people are foundational characteristics of a Gospel movement. If people become a bother, if Christians isolate themselves from others, the movement of the Gospel will cease. But God's love never fails. Whitney discovered that. She was baptized not long after she marched through her school hallways and invited people to her church. But she wasn't baptized alone. She stood with two friends who accepted her invitation that day at school, and, together, they received the gift of new life through "the washing of regeneration and renewal of the Holy Spirit" (Titus 3:5). Family members and friends celebrated with the group of eighth grade girls as they confessed their faith and celebrated that, in Christ, they were new creations. The love of Christ compelled someone to care about Whitney. It compelled Whitney to care about people in her life. This is the first marker of Gospel DNA. It needs to receive intense focus and ongoing prayerful consideration. Love for people cannot be underestimated as a critical God-given Gospel DNA marker. But the next marker may call for even greater courage and humility.

Questions for Discussion – Chapter Five

1. What points of practical action stood out to you in this chapter?

2. Read Ephesians 4:2-3. What work needs to be done in your life and in your community of faith to grow in kindness to one another and to grow in handling disputes well?

3. Discuss the questions at the bottom of page 52.

Gospel DNA Journal:

How might my church take another step in caring about each other, the community and the world…

How is God directing me to care about the people in my life in the name of Jesus…

Gospel DNA

DNA Marker Two: Multiplication

Chapter Six
Love Multiplies

"Jesus said, 'Go home to your friends and tell them how much
the Lord has done for you, and how he has had mercy on you.'
And he went away and began to proclaim in the Decapolis how
much Jesus had done for him, and everyone marveled."
Jesus to the formerly demon-possessed man in Mark 5:19–20

Endless Love

I'll never forget the worry that gripped me when my wife and I were expecting our second child. We had experienced two remarkable years with our first daughter. It was miraculous to welcome a new life into the world, to see her grow, and to bond so joyfully and profoundly with this new human being who was our very own. Love took on new meaning as we were now a family and as we poured our lives into our firstborn, our precious daughter.

Now another baby was on the way. We were thrilled. We were thankful. Our family was growing! But I wondered deep inside: How will I be able to love another child as much as I love the child we have? Will there be enough love to go around? Will our second child be shortchanged, somehow, as my wife and I divide our resources to give the attention, time and love she would need? Did having another child mean splitting up our love and doing the best we can with fewer resources?

Those worries coursed through my heart and mind until our second daughter was born. I'll never forget buckling her into her car seat for the ride home and coming to the delightful realization that love doesn't have to be divided; love multiplies!

I loved both my daughters fully—one hundred percent each. With my second daughter's birth, the reservoir of love and care in my heart and soul doubled! Miraculously, more love appeared. And it wasn't a duplication of the love for my first daughter. This was a unique connection, a singular heart and affection for a new little human being brought into our lives. Love never had to be divided, rationed, or reserved for later use. Love multiplies.

The church can worry just like I did. If it reaches out, if it starts new congregations, if it shares its resources, if it sends people, if it invests in its community, or if it multiplies ministry, will the reserves somehow dry up? Will there not be enough people, money, time, energy or know-how to pull everything off? Will people's ability to serve be divided and will everything come crashing down? It might be better, the people of God may assert, if we do all we can to maintain the status quo and manage growth according to our readiness and current resource levels.

This sounds very reasonable. But if I followed this advice, I would only have one child.

I met a remarkable woman at a park when my children were little. She was pushing her little girl on the swings and so was I. We struck up a conversation. She asked me how many children I had. I answered, "Two." I followed with the typical comments: "It's a big job. We keep very busy. There are lots of demands, but we are so thankful. We wouldn't trade it for the world." Of course, I then asked the same question in return: "How many children do you have?" She responded, "Thirteen."

Thirteen! Thirteen! I couldn't believe it. She was actually standing upright and smiling. She was wide awake and mobile. Thirteen children! I immediately congratulated her and told her she was a hero among parents, a wise and noble sage among mothers.

This woman loved children. She loved being a mom. She said that she had been changing diapers constantly for more than twenty years. No sets of twins were involved. By the time her youngest would enter kindergarten, her sleepless, hectic, wall-to-wall busy life with kids at home would total more than thirty years. If this woman decided to wait to have children until her energy level was ready and her bank account was full, she would have never made it to thirteen children. She probably would have not made it to one child. But she discovered that love does not have to be divided. Love multiplies.

Gospel DNA: Multiplication

That's the truth I see demonstrated every day in the lives and hearts of missionaries, followers of Jesus, and multiplying churches and networks. God hasn't shortchanged anyone. He hasn't run out of love for people who need Him and He hasn't put a cap on who could be a part of His Kingdom. God provides, opens doors, raises up new leaders, and creates new ministry opportunities that surprise me, delight me, and sometimes make me very nervous.

A friend of mine who is a mission network leader in a major urban area of the United States has helped start thirty new churches in the past dozen years or so. One of those new churches was started because the husband of a college professor drove his wife to work through a terribly dangerous and gang-ridden neighborhood every day. Finally, his heart was stirred and he knew that God wanted him to do something in that broken area of the city. He got connected to my friend, entered into training and discipleship, arranged to rent a small home on one of the blocks he drove past each day, and started a church. He reached out to the neighbors and began to connect with the community. There is much work yet to do there, but the presence of the church, the love and care from God's people, and the constructive spirit of Christ are changing people's lives. Who would have ever imagined a community of faith in a such a place?

Because of the church planting momentum in his network, my friend is concentrating on replicating himself by raising up and mentoring new servants of Jesus who will do exactly what he is doing among their own unique relationship networks. He has learned that God's love leads to multiplication.

That same spirit exists among a small group of missionaries who serve in one of the poorest and most dangerous regions in the nation. This border area is filled with violence, struggle, fear, a lack of resources and all the challenges that come with an undocumented existence in our country. But in the midst of this struggle, work is being done to equip middle school children with the Gospel of Jesus Christ and deploy them as leaders who bring the Good News to their families and friends. This creative focus on young people is bearing fruit as kids who are blessed by and excited about Jesus lead groups of their peers in discipleship gatherings and serving opportunities. Disciples and leaders are being multiplied as the news of hope in Christ spreads like wildfire through a community that needs Him desperately. New churches are springing up and more are on the way, but they are unlike traditional churches. When a church develops from a group of junior high students, how does it fit into our traditional organizational structures? But regardless of structure, young people keep gathering, hearing the Gospel, sharing it with others, and serving the community.

Love multiplies. God's love multiplies. His body, the church that bears His love, multiplies. Multiplication is a consistent marker of Gospel DNA. I saw it in my own denomination as it added an average of one new church EVERY WEEK for the first ONE-HUNDRED YEARS of its existence. I shouldn't be surprised. The DNA of multiplication is built into the Gospel message itself.

In Isaiah 49 God said, "It is too light a thing that you should be my servant to raise up the tribes of Jacob and to bring back the preserved of Israel; I will make you as a light for the nations, that my salvation may reach to the end of the earth" (Isaiah 49:6). The Good News of the Savior God was designed to multiply. Jesus commanded His disciples in Mark chapter 16, "Go into all the world and proclaim the gospel to the whole creation" (Mark 16:15). To the little and powerless band of disciples from the sticks, this was a bold and audacious mandate. The world? The whole creation? But multiplication was built into the Gospel. Jesus promised His disciples before He ascended into heaven, "But you will receive power when the Holy Spirit has come upon you, and you will be my witnesses in Jerusalem and in all Judea and

Samaria, and to the end of the earth" (Acts 1:8). The Gospel would spread far and wide. In 2 Timothy chapter 2, the Apostle Paul urged Timothy to live a life of multiplication: "What you have heard from me in the presence of many witnesses entrust to faithful men who will be able to teach others also" (2 Timothy 2:2). The Gospel DNA of multiplication propelled the proliferation of disciples, churches, and leaders. The Apostle John saw God's multiplying work in the Revelation vision: "Then I saw another angel flying directly overhead, with an eternal gospel to proclaim to those who dwell on earth, to every nation and tribe and language and people" (Revelation 14:6). Gospel DNA has multiplication as a key marker. Multiplication is what the church does.

A Multiplying Church

Why *wouldn't* we want a multiplying church? We could be afraid of the risks and potential lack of control. We may be comfortable and not want to expend the effort a multiplying church calls for. We may be distracted by internal arguments and wounds that make us fearful to venture out again. We may be deceived by myths and untruths about the nature of the Gospel or Christ's Church. But I believe today's generation craves the multiplication DNA of the Gospel. This is a generation that understands the power of multiplication. Crowd funding allows worthy causes to be resourced through grass roots efforts. Paying it forward and making a difference are becoming more important than personal comfort and gain. "Going viral" is a phenomenon that bypasses traditional marketing efforts and puts message multiplication in the hands of people on the street. Instead of participating in slick marketing, people share. People network. Grass roots multiplication is not only a familiar phenomenon, but one that is seen as authentic.

The body of Christ has what a new generation deeply desires. It is a living and breathing, sharing and difference-making organism created by God to bring renewed hope and eternal life to the world. Early believers behaved like people on social media today. Even in the face of threats, they said, "For we cannot help speaking about what we have seen and heard" (Acts 4:20 NIV). They had to share. This was organic, Spirit-embedded multiplication. By 100 A.D. there were as few as 25,000 Christians. Just over two-hundred years later, Christians numbered up to 20 million![28] All of this happened in spite of the lack of fully developed organizational and structural systems. Author and missiologist Alan Hirsch noted that early Christians had no church buildings as we know them, did not possess an established Scriptural canon, did not have settled forms of leadership, had no ministry programs or educational institutions, made joining the church very difficult, and were an illegal religion under the early Roman Empire.[29] Human odds were against the early church. But God's love cannot help but multiply. This is the DNA of the Gospel and the DNA of the church.

It is also good for the church. If you think that sending leaders, starting new ministries, and planting multiplying churches depletes a local ministry, think again. In a study of church planting released by LifeWay Research, new churches that multiplied and supported multiplication exhibited stronger growth than churches that did not focus on intentional multiplication. Average church attendance for new churches that started another congregation within three to five years was more than twice that of church plants that did not start a new congregation. The same was true for new churches that financially contributed to new church plants and mentored new leaders.[30] Intentional multiplication is good for the church. Church planting congregations know that planting leads to growth and vibrancy.

Multiplication is good for God's Kingdom, too. It's no secret that as churches mature, they can become insulated from people who don't yet know Jesus. Established churches have a more difficult time connecting with new people. For churches

---

[28] Alan Hirsch with Darryn Altclass., *The Forgotten Ways Handbook* (Grand Rapids: Brazos Press, 2009), 28.

[29] Hirsch, *The Forgotten Ways Handbook*, 29.

[30] Ed Stetzer, Micah Fries and Daniel Im, *"The State of Church Planting in the U.S"* (Nashville: LifeWay Research and NewChurches.com, 2015), 10-11.

under three years of age, it takes just ten people to to see one new person come to faith in Christ. For churches over fifteen years of age, it takes thirty-three people to do the same.[31] This is not all bad. Churches become families. They grow into groups that care for each other, mature in discipleship together, keep one another accountable and develop abiding friendships. They know and accept each other. But it isn't easy for new people to enter these families. As time goes by, churches become closed groups—no matter how hard they try to reach out. That's why new churches are needed. New communities of faith need to be started so more people can experience the beauty of being part of the body of Christ. The established church needs to give new people a chance to know Jesus and the new life He gives. It needs to embrace the fact that new things reach new people.

Compounding the issue of the church's effectiveness in reaching new people, Christian churches in America are becoming less accessible to the growing population. In 1900 there were twenty-eight churches for every ten-thousand Americans.[32] By 2014 that number decreased to only eleven churches for every ten-thousand Americans.[33] The United States needs more churches. Fortunately, there is hope. For the first time in many years, the number of new church plants in the United States outpaced the number of churches that closed. According to the 2015 study by LifeWay Research, *The State of Church Planting in the U.S.*, more than 4,000 new churches were started in 2014 compared to 3,700 churches that closed.

Could this indication of church multiplication momentum in the U.S. signal a shift toward a Gospel movement? Can the Gospel DNA of multiplication take hold to cause what some say is impossible for the Christian Church in the western world at this time in history?

---

[31] Ed Stetzer, *Planting Missional Churches* (Nashville: B&H Publishing Group, 2006). 8.

[32] Stetzer, *Planting*, 9.

[33] "Fast Facts About American Religion." Accessed March 28, 2016. http://hirr.hartsem.edu/research/fastfacts/fast_facts.html.

Questions for Discussion – Chapter Six

1. What new thoughts and insights about multiplication did this chapter stimulate in you?

2. What might cause you to be afraid or hesitant about reaching new people and starting new ministry?

3. Read Isaiah 49:5-6. Talk about why multiplication is good for the church and for God's Kingdom. Discuss why it might be good for your church, too.

4. Discuss how you are multiplying followers of Jesus in your life as well as ministry leaders of all ages in your church. What might you be able to do to improve the way you are developing new servants of Jesus?

5. Talk about your foundational motivation for reaching people with the Good News of Jesus and multiplying servant-leaders, ministries and churches.

Gospel DNA Journal:

What multiplication possibilities exist at my church…

How reaching new people with the Gospel is a joyful endeavor…

Marker Two: Multiplication
Chapter Seven
Gospel Movements

"For not only has the word of the Lord sounded forth from you
in Macedonia and Achaia,
but your faith in God has gone forth everywhere…"
The Apostle Paul in 1 Thessalonians 1:8

Is a Gospel Movement Possible?

A daunting challenge was presented to my colleagues and I when we teamed up in ministry as mission strategists in Texas. We were given the assignment to facilitate a mission movement in our region. The task seemed impossible because, at this time in the United States, a Gospel movement does not exist. There are some bright spots of multiplication and outreach, but on the whole, the Christian Church in America is in decline.[34] Compounding our conundrum was the fact that our denomination was in a serious stall. Let me clarify that: not a stall, a precipitous free-fall. Over the past fifteen years, the baptized membership of the LCMS dropped a whopping twenty percent. The most recent statistics show that the average worship attendance nationwide dropped fourteen percent in just one year.[35] To make matters worse, my church body comprises just 0.6% of the population of the United States. We're not well-known; we're not influential; and we're not in the mainstream conversation of American Christianity. Please understand, I am very thankful for my denomination and I've been blessed and inspired by remarkably dedicated and caring people in our church body over the past three decades of ministry. The LCMS continues to make a wonderful Gospel difference locally

---

[34] "America's Changing Religions Landscape," (Pew Forum).
[35] "LCMS congregations report statistics for 2014,"
https://blogs.lcms.org/2015/statistics-for-2014.

and around the world. But, let's face it: we're not a powerhouse and we're not growing. So we had our work cut out for us.

That's why I decided to start studying church planting movements. I believed the Holy Spirit could start a movement from my little tribe. After all, God is all about using small and marginalized people from out of the way places to accomplish significant Kingdom tasks. He's a "mustard seed" God. Nothing is impossible with Him. He chose the people of Israel to turn the world to the God of Heaven. His base of operations was the wilderness. He decided that little towns like Bethlehem and Nazareth would be His epicenters of divine activity. He arrived on earth as a baby, recruited twelve underachievers as disciples, and was overpowered and killed by angry church leaders. But He rose from the dead. When He did, the first witnesses were frightened moms and a former prostitute. Nevertheless, Jesus changed the world and started a movement of faith unmatched in all of history. So, yes, I saw my denomination in a perfect position to be used by God. If He did anything through us, He would receive all the glory for unleashing a movement of the Gospel. We couldn't claim any credit at all. But I needed to do some homework. What were the characteristics of Gospel movements? Were any church planting movements happening around the world today? If so, what could we learn from them that might catalyze an exponential multiplication movement among us? Could we be used by God to bring the gift of eternal life in Jesus Christ to an ever-expanding network of believers, disciples, leaders, churches and church multiplication networks? If so, how did we need to change, what did we need to adapt, and where did we need to start? Most importantly, have the characteristics of a church planting movement ever been present in the United States and, if they have, might it be possible to tap into this existing Gospel DNA in order to renew our own unique and contextual movement today?

Worldwide Gospel Movements

One of the foremost authorities on Gospel movements around the world is Dr. David Garrison, the Southern Baptist

International Mission Board's Global Strategist for Evangelical Advance. His book, *Church Planting Movements*, examined eight regions around the world and outlined the key characteristics found in multiplying movements of the Christian faith. The global south is fertile ground for the multiplication of the church today and Garrison found vibrant exponential growth in the Christian Church in Asia, Africa, the Middle East and South America. He defines a church planting movement as: "A rapid multiplication of indigenous churches planting churches that sweeps through a people group or population segment."[36] "Indigenous" means generated from within. Rapid growth means that the development of the church outpaces population growth as a people group is reached. A people group can include ethnicities in a region, the population of a country, or cultural segments in a particular area. If churches are being established at a rate that surpasses the ability of leaders to keep up with it, a movement is happening. Multiplication is happening not only when churches give birth to new churches, but when those new churches give birth to additional churches. The same is true for the multiplication of leaders and disciples. David Garrison identified ten characteristics common to every church planting movement he observed:

1. Extraordinary Prayer
2. Abundant Evangelism
3. Intentional Planting of Reproducing Churches
4. The Authority of God's Word
5. Local Leadership
6. Lay Leadership
7. House Churches
8. Churches Planting Churches
9. Rapid Reproduction
10. Healthy Churches[37]

---

[36] David Garrison, *Church Planting Movements, How God Is Redeeming a Lost World* (WIGTake Resources, LLC, 2012), Kindle Edition, Locations 247-248.
[37] Garrison, Kindle Location 2621

When I examined Dr. Garrison's observations and reviewed his list, I started to recall historical accounts of my denomination. His observations aligned with what I studied about the rapid growth of ethnically German churches of the Missouri Synod during the 1800s in the United States. The key markers of church planting movements around the world today lined up with the early twentieth century growth in Lutheranism, as well. But it wasn't just Lutheranism. The United States experienced a surge of church planting in a number of Christian denominations and among many ethnicities during the nineteenth and twentieth centuries. It appeared to me that America had some deep roots in the area of Gospel movements.

Let's make sure we offer clarity in the face of some possible fear and confusion, however. Garrison is careful to contrast Church Planting Movements and the Church Growth Movement. While the Church Growth Movement of the latter half of the twentieth century focused on large churches, receptive contexts for the Gospel and resourcing responsive areas with missionaries from the outside, Church Planting Movements tend to develop smaller churches among marginalized people with indigenous leadership.[38] It is important that this distinction is noted carefully. Growth in the church does not necessarily point to Church Growth principles and a Church Growth mindset. In fact, the Gospel movements of the 1800s and early 1900s bear a remarkable resemblance not to Church Growth methodology, but to the characteristics of Church Planting Movements. "Smaller churches among marginalized people with indigenous leadership" describes very well the German immigrant-based development of churches that became part of the LCMS. While Church Growth techniques may have commanded the limelight of church development and expansion in the 1960s, 70s and 80s, the substantive presence of Gospel DNA preceded the Church Growth trend and displayed what the Holy Spirit could do in a uniquely North American context.

---

[38] Garrison, *Church Planting Movements*, Kindle Location 303-335.

Another authority on Gospel movements is Steve Addison. He serves as Director of MOVE, an Australian based mission agency that multiplies disciples and churches. Addison's book, *Movements That Change the World: Five Keys to Spreading the Gospel*, broke Gospel movements down into five demonstrated characteristics:

1. White-Hot Faith
2. Commitment to a Cause
3. Contagious Relationships
4. Rapid Mobilization
5. Adaptive Methods[39]

It is important to see the characteristics of Gospel movements around the world today. These are markers of God's Kingdom work among His people. If we can observe God's consistent patterns of work to grow His Church, we may be able to discern how God is leading us in our own context.

Dwight Marable of Missions International devoted ten years of research to survey and evaluate church planting practices and theory in two nations where Gospel movements were evident. In his report, "Root Principles of Movements," Marable articulated seven root principles identified as crucial to the rapid reproduction of the church:

1. Intentional Reproduction
2. Continual Training
3. Simple Leadership
4. Relational Empowerment
5. Strategic Networking
6. Immediate Obedience
7. Passionate Prayer[40]

---

[39] Steve Addison, *Movements That Change the World: Five Keys to Spreading the Gospel* (Intervarsity Press, 2011), Kindle Edition, 22-23.
[40] Dwight Marable, "A Comparison of Root Principle Scores in 2 Recently Assessed Nations," *Missions International* (2010): 3-4.

These lists intentionally focus on methods and principles at work in Church Planting Movements. Upon closer examination of the Christian Church's development in the United States from the mid 1800s through the mid 1900s—particularly the Lutheran Church–Missouri Synod, another key dimension of Gospel movements becomes clear. Beneath the outward actions and practices of the movement, there is a foundational grace-based DNA given by God as a gift and developed by the work of the Holy Spirit through God's Word and sacraments. Intentional methods are an integral part of Gospel movements, but that intentionality is a result of how the church has been hard-wired by God, how He implanted Gospel DNA into His people that manifested itself in consistent characteristics. Gospel DNA is less "how to" than "what is" as a result of God's gracious work through His Word and Spirit. This was especially evident because a significant percentage of the founders of the Missouri Synod came to the United States not to reach out with the Gospel or to multiply churches, but to isolate themselves in their culture and tradition. A number of the organizers of the LCMS had no initial intention to reach a new nation with the Gospel, but God shook them from their deliberate separation and did something that surprised them. A careful study of the LCMS over its first one-hundred years revealed the characteristics of a uniquely American Gospel movement. These characteristics form the outline of this book:

People
Multiplication
Truth
Adaptability
Self-sacrifice

What do these characteristics tell us?

People: God moved the hearts of His followers to passionately yearn for the eternal salvation of the people of this nation. As you've seen already in the first section of this book, one refrain that occurs over and over again in the literature of my own denomination is "the love of souls." The Gospel movements of the late 1800s and the early to mid 1900s were fueled by servants of God—a church—that cared deeply about people. The strong theme that saturated every area of church life was a zeal for Christ's calling to reach the lost. People mattered. Their eternities mattered.

Multiplication: The church multiplied. It was intent on starting new churches, developing new leaders, sending new workers, and creating new partnerships—all for the sake of the proliferation of the Gospel. Multiplication was the result of a healthy church. It was the norm for the church. No community was to be without a community of faith. No person was to be separated from access to God's Word and sacraments. As the frontier expanded and as population grew, the church extended its reach further so no one would be without the saving Gospel of Jesus Christ.

Truth: Biblical doctrine and confession were never compromised. In fact, the solid and uncompromised truth of the Scriptures is what propelled the movement forward. The church— God's people—had a message to share. The message did not exist simply to be protected; it was given to be promoted, promulgated, and proclaimed. The presence of God's Truth was central and foundational to the movement of that Truth through His people to others.

Adaptability: While the church strongly resisted compromise of doctrine, it embraced flexibility in order to accomplish the mission of God. Some changes were easy and self-evident; some were born out of necessity and a changing context, some were grudgingly accepted in the face of strong traditions. But every change happened under the recognition that the mission of God needed to prevail over human desires and preferences.

Self-Sacrifice: This is another way of expressing people's love and care for the eternal welfare of all. The Holy Spirit moved men and women to sacrifice their personal welfare, their livelihoods, their families, and even their own lives in order to bring the Gospel to people who didn't know Jesus. Gospel DNA reflects Christ's own sacrifice. That DNA was evident in the early Gospel movements of the United States.

You will hear more about each of these areas as you make your way through this book. You will read remarkable stories of insight, leadership, love and commitment. God used these DNA markers to form His Church and to spread the Gospel in a growing nation. This is the DNA from which we can learn and, perhaps, by God's grace, it is the DNA with which we can reconnect. We desperately need to do so. The context of the United States has puzzled church leaders for the past half century. We don't know what to do. We wonder if we have to wait for everything to come crashing down in order to become truly effective again. But I wonder if God in His wisdom and grace created particular Gospel DNA in our context that worked once to cause a powerful expansion of His church—and can work again. Perhaps we are being called not to figure out new methods or imitate global phenomena, but to remember—as Jesus urged the church in Ephesus: "Remember therefore from where you have fallen; repent, and do the works you did at first" (Revelation 2:5).

When I studied what happened in my own church body, I became even more convinced that what the church needs in our nation today may be right under our noses.

Questions for Discussion – Chapter Seven

1. What was new to you as you read about characteristics of Gospel movements around the world and in the early years of the United States?

2. God works in small ways to do great things. How does this give you confidence in your life and ministry?

3. Look at the four lists of Gospel movement characteristics. Discuss which items resonate with you and how you would like them to take root in your church and community.

4. Read 2 Timothy 2:1-2. What is Paul saying in this verse? How might you be able to foster "movement thinking" as a Christian and as a church? Discuss how you can incorporate multiplication ideas into your life and ministry.

5. Love and care for people underlies Gospel movement efforts. How do you see God's love in Jesus Christ behind the lists of movement characteristics from Garrison, Addison, and Marable?

Gospel DNA Journal:

How I see characteristics of a Gospel movement in my church...

How the Holy Spirit is leading us to grow in movement thinking and action...

Marker Two: Multiplication
Chapter Eight
A DNA Discovery

"I make it my ambition to preach the gospel, not where Christ has already been named, lest I build on someone else's foundation."
The Apostle Paul in Romans 15:20

A DNA Discovery

Any of us born after 1950 may not remember it very well, but energetic evangelism, determined outreach, and rapid church planting was the norm in the Lutheran Church–Missouri Synod for its first century of existence. My denomination is indelibly marked with the DNA of multiplication. In its first hundred years, from 1847 to 1947, the LCMS grew from just twelve congregations to 5,240 congregations and from 4,000 people at the close of 1847 to more than 1.5 million souls by the end of 1947. This growth did not happen by accident. It was the result of Gospel DNA formed by God and embedded by the Holy Spirit into the church. The statistics are staggering.

Between 1847 and 1870, the United States population grew by 8.7 percent. During that same time, the LCMS grew by 96 percent. If we count those first twenty-three years as a spike in growth due to formation, the decades that follow continue to tell the story of a Gospel movement. Consider the decade by decade growth below:

U.S. Population Growth	LCMS Growth
1880: 23%	41.2%
1890: 20.3%	77%
1900: 17.4%	27%

Let's stop here. The history of the Lutheran Church–Missouri Synod shows the existence of two distinct Gospel movements. The first is from 1870 through about 1917. During this period of time, the LCMS was adding, on average, about two churches every week. During some years in the 1870s, 80s, and 90s a new church was added every other day. Between the late 1860s and the late 1870s the LCMS doubled in size (roughly 60,000 souls to 120,000 souls). Baptisms went from just over 9,000 each year to about 20,000 annually. This was a season of massive German immigration to the United States. Between 1850 and 1900 up to 150,000 Germans were arriving in the United States every year. The fledgling LCMS church was in the right place at the right time to reach the influx of German-speaking people. And the church chose to reach out.

The German immigrants were not compliant, church-going prospects looking for Lutheran congregations. They were a disparate group from many regions in a not yet unified Germany. They were from a variety of faith backgrounds and did not always have a positive inclination toward the church. Missionary John Detzer sailed to the United States in 1845. He was a German baker who heard the call to reach people with the Gospel in America. Detzer started eighteen churches in Ohio during his fifty-eight years of service. He commented on the audience he encountered while he simultaneously served three congregations and four preaching stations:

> Various listeners come, partly such as have never subscribed to a Christian confession, partly such as belong to diverse sects. With such people, who are wholly ignorant, we must have much patience. I preach as well as I can, as often as the Lord gives me grace; I spare no pains to go to the most forsaken places, to which the worst paths often lead; I let the Lord take care of the rest. Yes, I would not spare even my health (which declined considerably in the last year) and my life if only these poor scattered people who have lived till now without Christianity might be gathering into congregations.[41]

---

[41] Meyer, *Moving Frontiers*, 104.

Pastor Edward Doering, a traveling preacher in the great Northwest during the 1880s, braved sub-zero temperatures, driving rainstorms, mountainous terrain, the lack of resources and resistance from people in order to seek souls for Christ. He said, "I find people everywhere, i.e., Germans, former Lutherans, backsliders, doubters, distressed, and spiritually indifferent. The soil is hard, very hard."[42]

In his book *Torch Bearers*, Lawrence Meyer reflected on the barriers overcome by early LCMS mission work: "A marvelous thing had been accomplished in bringing about a harmonious community of Saxons, Hanoverians, Pomeranians, Schleswig-Holsteiners, etc. The petty provincialism which had not only kept them apart in Germany, but had militated for centuries against a united Germany, had been overcome in the church organization of the Missouri Synod."[43]

Multiplication

The development of the church in the United States was not a "build it and they will come" proposition. People weren't knocking down the doors of churches in order to join or having so many children that pastors simply had to line them up in the sanctuary for baptisms and membership. The United States was a mission field. It was a multi-ethnic epicenter of Christian outreach as the population exploded with new residents. Some groups, the LCMS included, decided to engage in evangelistic outreach among the new arrivals. Other groups decided that outreach to new immigrants wasn't important. English speaking religious denominations in the United States dominated the religious landscape in the late 1700s. The Congregationalist, Episcopal, and Presbyterian Churches did not make a shift to reach new immigrants in their own languages. Methodists and Baptists, however, began aggressive efforts to reach ethnic groups.

---

[42] Hans Spalteholz, Matthew L. Becker and Dwain Brandt, Eds. *God Opens Doors: A Centennial Celebration of the Northwest District of The Lutheran Church–Missouri Synod* (Portland: Northwest District of the LCMS, 2000), 33.
[43] L. Meyer, *Torch Bearers*, 13.

Religious adherence shifted dramatically between the late 1700s and the mid 1800s. In some regions of the U.S., adherence to the Congregational Church was 60% of the population in 1776. Only 8% of the people claimed to be Baptist or Methodist. By 1850, only 19% claimed to be Congregational while 58% claimed to be Baptist or Methodist. Roman Catholics began to reach out to the new immigrants, as well. Breaking away from the traditional geographic parish arrangement, the Roman Catholic Church began to form churches around language and nationality. By 1916 nearly half of all Catholic faith communities in the United States held worship services in a language other than English.[44]

Ethnic outreach in language and in cultural gatherings escalated during the peak immigration years. The new LCMS found itself using the same evangelistic tool other denominations were using during this time of rapid growth in the U.S. My denomination didn't intentionally embark on an ethnic evangelistic strategy. The Missouri Synod was simply here at the right time and in the right place—by God's grace—with a zeal to share the Gospel with fellow Germans. The DNA of multiplication became rooted in the LCMS as it began what Dr. Larry Rast, President of Concordia Theological Seminary in Fort Wayne, Indiana, calls an inclusive effort toward cultural Germans. This is an important point. Speaking German and embracing German cultural traditions was not meant to exclude people from this emerging Gospel movement. On the contrary, the German language and traditions were utilized to embrace a wide variety of people with the love of Jesus Christ and to connect them to the community of believers. Even the long and cumbersome name of the LCMS at that time shouted inclusiveness: "The German Evangelical Lutheran Synod of Missouri, Ohio and Other States." Germans—the hundreds of thousands streaming through U.S. ports—were welcome! Those who needed the Gospel were welcome! People from the burgeoning western growth corridor of the nation were welcome! People from many regions were welcome!

---

[44] *Encyclopedia of American History.* Gale Encyclopedia of U.S. History, The Gale Group, Inc. 2006.

The multiplication DNA of the LCMS was so strong during this time, the percentage growth surpassed that of the Methodist Church—one of the most vibrant Church Planting Movements of the 1800s. Walther, Wyneken and their cohorts were in their wheelhouse as the compulsion for Gospel outreach pulsed through their veins. Remember how David Garrison defined a Church Planting Movement: "A rapid multiplication of indigenous churches planting churches that sweeps through a people group or population segment." The LCMS in the 1800s was a classic Church Planting Movement, similar to ethnic movements happening in the Global South today. Garrison added: "Though the rate varies from place to place, Church Planting Movements always outstrip the population growth rate as they race toward reaching the entire people group."[45] That's exactly what happened in the LCMS. And that's the trend that continued after a pause in the early 1900s.

The Next Wave

We'll explore the "pause" in LCMS growth and how to overcome a pause in the next chapter, but after a lull in growth, the LCMS began a second Gospel Movement, a uniquely American Evangelistic movement. The statistics tell the story:

U.S. Population Growth	LCMS Growth
1910: 17.4%	17.1%
1920: 28%	13%
1930: 14%	13.2%
1940: 6.8%	13.3%
1950: 12.3%	22.3%
1960: 16%	30%

Multiplication of churches slowed from 1917 to about 1937. On average, only one church was added every two weeks during that time period. But from the late 1930s through the early 1960s, the pace quickened again. A new church was being added

---

[45] Garrison, *Church Planting Movements*, Kindle Locations 260-261.

on average every four and a half days. Two churches were being started each week during some shorter periods within this timeframe. Was the growth due to the baby boom after the war? Statistics and historical evidence tell a different story. The Gospel movement called "Missouri" was outpacing population growth in the United States. Year by year it was comprising a greater percentage of the U.S. population. Multiplication was at work— the multiplication of believers, of disciples, of leaders and of churches.

The April 7, 1958 edition of Time Magazine featured Lutheranism on its cover. The article noted that new Lutheran congregations were springing up at a rate of one every 54 hours. Two-million Lutherans were added to American Lutheranism in the previous ten years. Zeroing in on the LCMS, the write-up commented: "Converts are pouring in, attracted by billboards, magazine ads, TV programs and, in the *Lutheran Hour*, the most widely broadcast sermon on radio (1,209 stations). A campaign of 'Preaching, Teaching, and Reaching,' organized by the Evangelical Lutheran Church is ringing doorbells and organizing study groups."[46]

This was a Gospel movement. Catalyzed by the *Lutheran Hour* radio program begun in the 1930s by Rev. Dr. Walter A. Maier and the Lutheran Laymen's League of the LCMS, the momentum of Gospel outreach was resulting in new believers and new churches throughout the United States and the world. The Lutheran Church–Missouri Synod, once a Gospel movement to German-speaking people, now became a thoroughly American church multiplication phenomenon. During this period of time, more than ten percent of the total congregations in the LCMS were preaching stations—new missions being developed in new communities for new people. Churches routinely had "mission services" on Sunday afternoons in far-flung places needing a church. Pastors and laypeople made treks to those communities in order to bring the Good News of Jesus to ones in need.

---

[46] "The New Lutheran," *Time*, April 7, 1958, 59.

"Preaching, Teaching, and Reaching" events were week-long "revivals" held in neighborhoods and hosted by a local congregation. Special speakers were brought in. Neighborhood canvasses and invitations were initiated by church members. Special evening gatherings for young people, women and men were held throughout the week—all for the purpose of sharing the Gospel.

LCMS President John Behnken commented in the Chicago Tribune "Religious News and Notes" section before the 1950 LCMS convention, "New Missouri synod churches have been organized at the rate of one new church in each three and a half days for the last three years in Canada and the United States. A new record for adult converts to the synod also was set in the triennium. Such rapid growth, with a half million adults expected to join within the decade, raises problems of staffing churches with pastors."[47]

In addition to the biological multiplication happening during the baby boom, spiritual multiplication was prolific in this, the second Gospel movement of the LCMS. Multiplication of believers, disciples, leaders and churches was normal activity. It was Gospel DNA from the Savior who lauds multiplication as the definitive characteristic of being faithful. Consider the parable of the talents.

In Matthew 25, Jesus described three servants entrusted with their master's riches. The first servant put the money to work and gained five additional talents (a "talent" was a measure of weight for precious metal). Multiplication was at work. The second servant was given two talents and gained two more. The third servant buried his master's money in the ground. His reason? When the master returned after a long time, the third servant explained, "Master, I knew you to be a hard man, reaping where you did not sow, and gathering where you scattered no seed, so I was afraid, and I went and hid your talent in the ground. Here you have what is yours" (Matthew 25:24–25). The master called the

---

[47] Rev. John Evans, "Religious News and Notes," *Chicago Tribune*, June 17, 1950.

first two servants "faithful": "Well done, good and faithful servant!" You've heard that verse before. Being faithful means multiplying what the master provides. Faithfulness is a joyful and exciting challenge. Multiplication is an energizing enterprise. Gospel DNA is marked with God's multiplying power and grace. What did the master call the servant who was afraid, who protected and preserved his money? He said to him, "You wicked and slothful servant!" (Matthew 25:26). Keeping the Gospel safe and not putting it to work for multiplication is considered lazy and evil behavior by God. These are sobering words for each of us who has been entrusted with Jesus' commission to preach the Good News to all creation (Mark 16:15). They are challenging words when we face a "pause" in growth and are tempted to withdraw and become afraid.

Questions for Discussion – Chapter Eight

1. What surprised you and stimulated your thinking in this chapter?

2. What did you learn about the heart and spirit of the church as you read the history of the LCMS's expansion? What made a significant impression on you?

3. What adjustments in our personal and church behavior today might help reinvigorate a culture of Kingdom multiplication?

4. At one time, it was normal for churches to have "mission services"—Sunday afternoon or weekday gatherings in communities where there was no church. What 21st-century version of that outreach might work for the people and communities around you?

5. Read the parable of the talents in Matthew 25:14-30. Talk about what it means to be faithful to God and how that relates to our love for Him and other people.

Gospel DNA Journal:

What fosters a climate of multiplication in the church...

How am I part of God's multiplication efforts...

Marker Two: Multiplication
Chapter Nine
What Being Faithful Really Means

"He who had received the five talents came forward, bringing five talents more, saying, 'Master, you delivered to me five talents; here I have made five talents more. His master said to him, 'Well done, good and faithful servant. You have been faithful over a little; I will set you over much. Enter into the joy of your master.'"
Jesus, telling the parable of the talents in Matthew 25:20–21

Multiplication Against the Odds

It was a chilly November day in downtown San Antonio. I stood in a hotel meeting room, telling some stories about how daring and entrepreneurial my denomination had been. The bold and passionate statements of our early leaders reflected fervent care about people's eternal welfare. The accounts showed that our forefathers were heroic in their strenuous efforts to start new churches for people who had no access to faith communities and for many who had never followed Christ. This is what today's generation yearns for. They are disillusioned with the institutional church. They don't want to be part of a self-serving, inward-looking, institutionally complex and resistant entity. They want to make a difference and be real.

About twenty people sat in the room. It was a breakout session at a conference. After the presentation was finished, a friend who had attended college with me but whom I hadn't seen in a long time approached me with tears in his eyes. He was now a pastor and professor. He had always been an enterprising and creative person. He was smart and consistently looked more deeply into ideas and issues. He said to me, "Mike, my grandfather was a pastor in Canada. He started over twenty churches. That's who we really are."

My friend had tears because he realized something was missing. Why weren't we looking beyond ourselves? How had we become so satisfied with the status quo? Why were we so afraid?

I did some digging. His grandfather may have been Rev. C.T. Wetzstein, a missionary pastor sent to Saskatoon. He was just twenty-seven years old when he began organizing new churches in 1914. He preached in bunkhouses and joined with families to start new worshipping communities in homes. There were no boundaries to the Gospel, and his energetic spirit was set free by a church that echoed the powerful Word of Jesus, "Go!"

After I presented at a church in Austin, Texas, a retired pastor approached me and told me about his grandfather. He was born in Germany in 1855. His parents brought him to the United States in 1869. Johann Friedrich Wilhelm Harms studied for the pastoral ministry under Dr. C.F.W. Walther at Concordia Seminary in St. Louis. He sat at the feet of the man who knew that an exclusive and insular spirit was deadly to the Church of Jesus Christ. So equipped, Harms started his ministry in Bancroft, Nebraska. He stayed there for his 57 years of ministry. But he didn't stop at serving the flock with faithfulness and care. Pastor Harms started four additional congregations. Pastor Walter Harms, the retired pastor who approached me, made a copy of his grandfather's funeral bulletin and sent it to me. He told me, "Take a look. In the midst of everything he did to serve his family and the church, he also did what was normal in his day. He extended the Kingdom into new communities. He started new churches." Multiplication was a standard marker of Gospel DNA.

The story of Texas is inspiring. The state was a mission outreach territory of the Southern District of the LCMS. Missionaries were sent not to become comfortable and busy parish pastors in one locality, but to start new faith communities where there was no access to the Gospel. The "normal" load carried by frontier pastors seems inconceivable today. Consider Pastors J.J. Trinklein and Fr. Wunderlich. Trinklein ordained and installed candidate Wunderlich in 1884. Immediately, Wunderlich assumed responsibility for multiple locations: "Pastor Wunderlich was made responsible for the preaching places between Waco and Houston... Arrangements were also made to have six of the newly developed preaching stations served by the pastors of established congregations...This left ten preaching places for Pastor Trinklein to serve while he continued to explore new areas."[48] If you haven't driven in Texas much, Waco and Houston are 182 miles apart! It takes three hours in a car to get from one place to another. Wunderlich covered that area with a horse! Trinklein's load *decreased* to only ten preaching places so he could explore new areas. The Gospel DNA of multiplication was standard operating procedure even when the odds were stacked against the church.

And the odds were certainly against the church in the United States between 1917 and 1937—the LCMS included. One blow after another caused a complete shift in the church's focus. With suddenness and pain, the church entered a pause.

The Pause Years

World War I brought massive and unexpected opposition to the German Evangelical Lutheran Synod of Missouri, Ohio and Other States. As the Kaiser plunged the world into war, anti-German sentiment exploded in the United States. The opposition to and suspicion of the German church were so strong, the Synod revised its constitution and dropped "German" from its name in 1917. The following year, the United States outlawed speaking and teaching German to young people in schools. Keep in mind, German was the second-most used language after English in the United States at the time. The decision was appealed and later overturned, but the damage was done. In an instant, German-speaking young people were told they had to memorize the catechism in the English language. Suddenly, the ethnically-based strategy for outreach with the Gospel was no longer tenable. The LCMS entered an identity crisis.

---

[48] Robert J. Koenig, *Pause to Ponder: A History of The Lutheran Church–Missouri Synod in Texas* (Texas District LCMS, 1980), 49.

At the same time, the armed forces drafted thousands of young men for service in the war. Many lost their lives. The 1937 Statistical Yearbook of the LCMS notes: "1919 is the only year in the history of our Synod in which a decrease in the number of souls had to be recorded. A decrease of 4,027 souls was caused by the drafting of thousands of our boys for the Army."[49] An additional blow was the flu pandemic in 1918. Its deadly impact killed 675,000 people in the U.S. alone. Then immigration laws were radically revised. The Emergency Immigration Act of 1921 dramatically restricted the number of immigrants to the U.S. By 1924 the number of immigrants entering the U.S. declined by 80%. If that wasn't enough, the birthrate began a steady decline. By 1920 the birthrate was nearly 25% lower than it was in the late 1800s. By 1930, it was cut in half.[50] Everything was changing. The Roaring Twenties brought the attraction of new technology, art and entertainment. At the same time, self-centered materialism, promiscuity and distraction began to hold sway. Urbanization shifted population centers away from rural life and community. Prohibition brought religious pietism and moralism to the surface while driving corruption and organized crime beneath a thin veneer of propriety. The Great Depression then plunged the nation into crippling poverty and gloom. Historian Dr. Robert Handy quoted Professor William Kelley Wright's assessment of the church during this challenging time. In the thick of the depression, Wright said, "Today we are passing through a period of religious depression not less severe than the concomitant moral and economic depression."[51]

What was the church to do? It stayed rooted in Gospel DNA.

---

[49] Statistics of the Missouri Synod 1847-1937. Compiled for the Saxon Immigration Centennial by Rev. E. Eckhardt, Part IV, note 22.

[50] Michael Haines, "Fertility and Mortality in the United States," https://eh.net/encyclopedia/fertility-and-mortality-in-the-united-states/.

[51] Robert T. Handy, "The American Religious Depression, 1925-1935," Church History, 29.1 (March 1, 1960): 3, http://search.proquest.com/openview /ff289c7e796d2935bebdf8d01fc6dd75/1?pq-origsite=gscholar

Consider some statements made by Rev. John H.C. Fritz in 1919. At the time, he was the Chairman of the Mission Board of the Western District of the LCMS and pastor of Bethlehem Lutheran Church in St. Louis. He wrote a little book called *The Practical Missionary.* In it, he said, "Every Christian is a missionary."[52] He went on to embrace the language trends—even if this meant grinning and bearing it: "While for obvious reasons, our Lutheran Church in this country did its work through the medium of a foreign language, it is of late years very rapidly coming to be an English-speaking church. For thirty-five years we have had congregations which used no other language than the language of our country. There is no doubt that the future of our Lutheran Church of this country belongs to the English-speaking Lutheran Church."[53] He then got to the heart of the matter: "A Lutheran missionary who ferrets out only the former Lutherans, or the people of a certain nationality, as those of German extraction, is not doing his mission work in accordance with his Lord's explicit directions. Christ, who died for all, would have us bring His Gospel of Salvation to all. The unchurched, that is, such as are not members of a Christian church, are the missionary's mission material. These the missionary will find everywhere."[54]

People mattered. Multiplication was the calling and challenge. Even Rev. E. Eckhardt, the editor of the LCMS Statistical Report in 1937, focused on Gospel DNA as he said, "Here is the place to say something about the declining birth-rate." He discussed the influx of immigrants, the increase of the LCMS when the English Synod joined the LCMS in 1911, and the restriction in the immigration laws. Then he commented with mission optimism: "On the other hand, the number of adults baptized and confirmed is rising from year to year."[55] Dr. Walter A. Baepler, professor and president of Concordia Theological

---

[52] John H.C. Fritz, *The Practical Missionary* (St. Louis: Concordia Publishing House, 1919), 3.

[53] Fritz, *The Practical Missionary*, 9.

[54] Fritz, *The Practical Missionary*, 12.

[55] Statistics of the Missouri Synod 1847-1937, note 24.

Seminary from 1936-1958, reinforced this mission outlook even during circumstances that caused consternation, confusion, and decline. He noted in the 100th anniversary historical account of the LCMS that in 1947, the Synod celebrated nearly 190,000 new adults who had confessed their faith at the altars of Missouri Synod churches since 1918.[56] That's more than 6,500 new adult believers on average every year for nearly thirty years—including lean years of decline. Every day for three decades, eighteen men and women confessed their faith in Jesus Christ for the first time at Lutheran altars.

Gospel DNA was at work. Multiplication was the focus. Youth efforts were ramped up in the 1920s as Dr. Walter A. Maier injected new excitement into the Walther League, a young people's organization that embodied the spirit of a multiplying church. Radio ministry was kicked off in 1930 as The Lutheran Hour radio show was started by, yes, Dr. Walter A. Maier. In 1929, seminary students teamed up with Dr. Walter A. Maier, a professor at Concordia Seminary in St. Louis at the time, to plant a church in the city—a student led laboratory of multiplication. Maier commented, "This mission would grow through converts, not Lutheran transferees."[57] The church was named "St. Stephen's" because, as Maier explained, "…Stephen's role as the first layman actively engaged in church work. This was to be a laymen's church, like Stephen, 'full of faith and the Holy Spirit,' a living example of how the 'royal priesthood of believers' could function at the heart of the inner city."[58]

What do you do during a pause? You stay faithful by continuing to put the Gospel to work. What do you wait and watch for during a pause? An open door of God's grace to take you to the next season. If you were faithful with little, God may allow you to be faithful with much. Walter A. Maier was a key part of the LCMS's open door. He was God's instrument to help

---

[56] Baepler, *A Century of Grace*, 357.

[57] Paul Maier, *A Man Spoke, a World Listened* (New York: McGraw Hill, 1963), 105.

[58] Maier, *A Man Spoke*, 108.

take the LCMS into a new season of vibrant ministry. Robert Koenig reflected on the impact Walter A. Maier and The Lutheran Hour had on the LCMS:

> The Lutheran Hour, which came into being in the early thirties, brought the message of free salvation through the crucified Christ into many homes, and many of these homes were non-Lutheran. As prejudices were dispelled, doors were opened. The Lutheran Church was no longer the church of immigrants from Germany and their descendants; it was rapidly becoming what it should always have been—the church through which the Good News of free salvation by God's grace in Christ was brought to everyone.[59]

What do you do during a pause? You resist the devil's attempt to make paralyzing fear the prevailing spirit, "for God gave us a spirit not of fear but of power and love and self-control" (2 Timothy 1:7). You refuse to believe that the church is not advancing, "for we walk by faith, not by sight" (2 Corinthians 5:7). You redouble efforts to share the Gospel, "For the word of God is living and active, sharper than any two-edged sword, piercing to the division of soul and of spirit, of joints and of marrow, and discerning the thoughts and intentions of the heart" (Hebrews 4:12). You receive what God is teaching you in the wilderness, "for though I am free from all, I have made myself a servant to all, that I might win more of them" (1 Corinthians 9:19). You keep putting the Gospel to work and you watch, because Jesus opens doors for us that no one can shut (Revelation 3:8).

---

[59] Koenig, *Pause to Ponder*, 74.

Questions for Discussion – Chapter Nine

1. How did the stories and statements of this chapter inspire you? What stood out most?

2. If your church seems to be in a "pause," what might be causing it? What open doors is God providing these days to bring you out of that pause?

3. According to this chapter, what do you do during a "pause" in ministry and life? Talk about what that might look like in your life and context.

4. What could it look like in your context to put the Gospel to work in a new way?

5. 1 John 4:18 says, "Perfect love casts out fear." How does God's love push fear away? How does the love He gives us for others bring us through obstacles that might stand in the way of sharing the Gospel?

Gospel DNA Journal:

How I can be faithful even when life seems paused...

How God is showing the way through and out of a pause (for me and my church) ...

Marker Two: Multiplication
Chapter Ten
How to Multiply

"And the things you have heard me say in the presence of many witnesses entrust to reliable men who will also be qualified to teach others."
The Apostle Paul in 2 Timothy 2:2 (NIV)

How to Multiply

Throughout the chapters of this section you've heard the refrain of multiplication and have encountered the daily work of ordinary believers to fuel an exponential movement of the Gospel. But what was normal three generations ago seems foreign and very difficult today. How do you reconnect with the Gospel DNA of multiplication? Doesn't it take too much time? Isn't it expensive? Isn't it risky? Will you set yourself up for failure? We respond that way because, to us, multiplication has become an additional activity. Instead of being the very fabric of life as a believer and as a church—normal behavior in every aspect of ministry, multiplication has become a separate category of thought, planning and strategy. It's an "over and above" budget item. It's a program. It is something a small group of church members might be interested in, but it is not the primary focus of the Christian life and the church.

You see how serious our disconnection from Gospel DNA has become.

That's why the first step in recovering the Gospel DNA of multiplication is to consider it normal again—part of everything we do, every plan we make, and every thought we think. If you're in an existing church or if you're planting a church, the first step to reengage with the multiplication marker of Gospel DNA is to SHARE.

Share

A close friend of mine and a very faithful follower of Christ commented to me about her Sunday morning worship experience, "It really felt like I went to church." Why? The music was beautiful. The hymns were familiar. The pastor preached a Biblical message. The order of service was similar to what she had grown up doing. Sometimes she would sing in the choir while her husband helped the usher team. It *felt* like church. After Sunday morning worship, she and her husband went out to lunch with a group of friends. They enjoyed a wonderful meal and joyful conversation. At home that afternoon, she relaxed with a nap while her husband watched the game on TV. It was a good Sunday. Monday would bring work and lists of things to do, but Sunday was a day of spiritual, physical and emotional restoration.

That's how the Sunday scenario plays out around our nation each weekend for the roughly 20% of people who feel it's important to attend a church service on a weekend. The routine makes the people happy and comfortable. They are glad to hear the faithful message of God's grace in Jesus Christ in a context that feels favorable for personal growth and learning. They're eager to serve and be a part of congregational life.

There's just one problem: We can easily fall into the habit of hoarding God's grace.

It is tempting and almost a default mode in our Christian lives to let the treasure of new life in Jesus stop with us. We soak in great sermons. We highlight verses in our Bibles and learn many new facts and insights in Bible study. We celebrate moving worship services. We enjoy the fellowship of small group ministry. We serve on mission trips and in a variety of church ministries. We move into church leadership and responsibility. We experience the transformation of the Holy Spirit and use our gifts to the glory of God. But too often, that's where the richness of God's new life stops. With us. We have lunch, go home and take a nap. We're glad about what we've experienced, but we don't think about how we may be able to include more people in these life-giving and life-enriching experiences given by God. We don't think about sharing.

What if every Christian became determined to involve someone outside the church in every faith activity? Are you going to pray? Ask someone to be your prayer partner. Are you going to study the Gospel of Matthew? Ask a co-worker to study it and talk about it with you. Are you going on a mission trip? Include a friend who may not know Jesus but who wants to make a difference in the world. Are you heading off to a women's retreat? Ask people who need some soul-refreshment to come along with you. Are you going to church and having lunch afterwards? Invite people God places in your life to come along and to enjoy lunch and conversation with you. Are you entering into a conversation? How can you share the hope you have in a natural and winsome way?

It may not be possible to do this in every situation, but if we set our sights on sharing God's blessings instead of having the benefit and blessing stop with us, we may become connected more deeply to the Gospel DNA of multiplication.

What if every church set out to make sure that at least 50% of the people involved in ministries were not from within the church walls? Is the church forming an usher team? Have each person invite someone to help bless people. Is it time for a church work day? Invite students who need community service hours to lend a hand. Are Sunday School or Vacation Bible School teachers being recruited? Ask each teacher to bring a friend who may be disconnected from the church to serve as a classroom assistant and accountability partner. Is the altar guild setting up for communion on the weekend? Bring along grandchildren and their friends to see, hear about, and help prepare for the special celebration on Sunday. Your pool of people resources does not end with the church membership list. God gives you the whole community to reach and invite.

This may get very challenging and even a bit messy, but if everyone is always asking, "Who else needs to hear this, be involved in this, and experience this?", multiplication may become normal again. People may come to know Jesus Christ and the blessing of new life in Him. The DNA of multiplication will be transmitted to every new relationship. A chain reaction of inviting and including will begin. The Gospel will not stop with us. Of course, that means you will have to do some searching.

Search

One of the few prayer requests Jesus gave His followers is found in Luke chapter 10. Jesus said to seventy-two Kingdom workers, "The harvest is plentiful, but the laborers are few. Therefore pray earnestly to the Lord of the harvest to send out laborers into his harvest" (Luke 10:2). Jesus asked His followers to pray that God would send workers for the great harvest of souls the Spirit is already preparing. More workers are needed. There are never enough. Why do we, then, practice solo ministry, act as if the job is much too difficult and complicated for others, shoulder the load ourselves without trying to work ourselves out of a job by giving as much ministry away as possible, and narrow the access to service in God's Kingdom with, at times, unreasonable, complicated and expensive requirements?

We need more workers. Jesus asked us to pray for a supply. We have to let the supply in.

When I started my current ministry, a wise man told me, "Find twelve disciples." He was underscoring the importance of multiplying new disciples who become new leaders. This is a standard strand of Gospel DNA. A leader is never meant to be a dead-end of Kingdom work; he or she is meant to be a new conduit for developing and sending new leaders.

I have to confess that as a pastor I was very busy with writing new messages, visiting the ill and hurting, planning new ministry initiatives, interfacing with community leaders, and teaching new people about Jesus. My life was very full. But two factors roused me from a selfish solo ministry pursuit. First, I couldn't do it all myself. I was getting beat up and tired out. There was no way I could accomplish the task of ministry alone. Sometimes God brings desperation and discomfort to teach important lessons. Second, wise and Spirit-led believers kept approaching me with the desire to serve. They wouldn't leave me alone. It took a while, but the message finally made its way through my thick skull: ministry is not about me; it is "to equip the saints for the work of ministry, for building up the body of Christ" (Ephesians 4:12).

I also have to confess that I'm a Baby Boomer. I'm at the tail end of a huge post-war generation that has been dominating the demographic landscape for years. We Baby Boomers have been notorious for not letting go, not making room, and not sharing. Life has been about us. As a consequence, younger generations and new leaders have been shut out of new opportunities because we keep holding on to our turf. We're healthy, living longer than the previous generation, and want to be in the limelight. So we keep hanging on. But God broke my grip in two ways. First, He placed before me a cadre of remarkable new leaders. I would be a poor and selfish steward to waste such gifts. Second, He showed me the consequence of not sharing and not handing off the baton: an aging and diminishing one-dimensional denomination that is quickly losing its relevance. This couldn't continue.

So I began arranging breakfast meetings with people who demonstrated leadership gifts and desires. We read Henri Nouwen's *In the Name of Jesus* and talked about what it meant to serve God's people. People developed ministry plans. They were released to practice doing new things. We served side by side, talked about the challenges and rigors of ministry, and dreamed about what God might accomplish. I searched for new disciples and sent new leaders. I determined to give every part of my ministry away—to end up with absolutely nothing to do, but every time I gave something away, God poured in much more. I realized that every Christian needs to ask, "Who am I developing as a worker in God's Kingdom? Who will not only take my place, but will surpass me in vision and ability? How am I giving ministry away? Who can't I reach that someone else can?" We're not that great at this in the church today. Either we want to be the star or we're afraid about what new people will bring. But we need the

Gospel DNA of multiplying leaders. We need new generations to reach new generations. We need ethnic leaders to reach ethnic communities. We need both men and women to be activated in serious and substantial ministry. We need the church to look like the people around us. We need workers for the great and plentiful harvest.

A key movement in mission has been the development of church multiplication networks. Local leaders who are passionate about a region search for new leaders who will be sent to use their particular gifts in order to make a Gospel impact among the people they can uniquely reach. Network organizers gather new leaders together for learning, accountability, discipleship, and sharpening. There is no stardom, only service to one another and sending for the high calling of the Gospel. A high percentage of churches being planted in the regions I serve are being planted through or with the help of church planting networks. These networks are signs of hope that selfishness and solo acts are coming to an end. The Gospel DNA of multiplication is taking hold. I encourage network thinking as churches and leaders contemplate new starts. Instead of going it alone in a region, banding together with others can foster a movement of the Gospel. If you'd like to find out more about networks or get connected to some network leaders, go to: http://txlcms.org/texas-partners-in-mission-many-church-planting-efforts/. But after sharing and searching, action has to happen.

Start

The time comes when you need to do something. Being ready and aiming has to stop at some time. The situation and circumstances may not be perfect, but if we never fire, we'll never make progress. If you're going to be a part of God's Gospel multiplication, you need to start new things: churches, ministries, missional communities, preaching stations, satellite sites, evangelistic outreach, prayer walks, community canvasses—something. You have to stop planning and start starting.

A retired church planter told me recently about a church he started that began worship services just two weeks after his arrival. Usually it takes months to initiate the first public worship gathering, but people in the area were ready. They started quickly, became dynamos of outreach, and rapidly began to grow and flourish as a church. Sometimes God works faster than you think He will. All you need to do is get started.

Multiplication means starting things. But it means much more than starting a one-hour worship meeting on Sunday morning. The church is much more than that. Remember what the new followers of Jesus did in the book of Acts:

They devoted themselves to the apostles' teaching and the fellowship, to the breaking of bread and the prayers. And awe came upon every soul, and many wonders and signs were being done through the apostles. And all who believed were together and had all things in common. And they were selling their possessions and belongings and distributing the proceeds to all, as any had need. And day by day, attending the temple together and breaking bread in their homes, they received their food with glad and generous hearts, praising God and having favor with all the people. And the Lord added to their number day by day those who were being saved (Acts 2:42–47).

That's more than a one-hour assembly. It's life! It is what people are craving today: meaning, connection, awe, and making a difference. It is a full life from the Savior. It is courage in the face of despair, hope that lasts forever, and sure footing in turbulent and uncertain times. What can you start that will bring the fullness of life in Christ to people God has placed in your life? What might God be starting that you need to get on board with?

A good place to begin is to ask some questions:
- Where is the Gospel needed in your context?
- How can you go to that context with the Gospel?
- Who might God be providing to help open a door into that context?

- How can you bring the fullness of all of God's gifts into what you've started (see Acts 2:42 again)?

My friend Dr. David Kim leads a mission network in the Houston area. He uses a "Good, Better, Best" continuum to describe starting new ministries. It is GOOD to make a difference. Holistic ministry to help meet people's felt and very genuine immediate needs shows the love of Jesus. It is BETTER to make relationships. Serving people should lead to genuine mutual relationships that demonstrate God's love and care. It is BEST to make disciples. Bringing the fullness of God's Word and sacraments to a context will transform people with God's grace. Those new followers of Christ will then be equipped to make more disciples. How will what you start ultimately develop more disciple-making disciples? You can find more of Dr. Kim's resources at: www.glocalmission.org.

Don't be afraid to try things and fail. We live in a day and age when we need new expressions of church. We need "embryonic" churches—gatherings of people who are beginning to receive and live out the beauty of God's grace and the deep meaning of the life He gives. Is God calling you to the lonely and lost in nursing homes? Go ahead and start something. Reach every elderly person in your community with Jesus' embracing love and hope. Is God directing you to families and children in your neighborhood? Go ahead and start something. Talk, eat, share, play. See what the Spirit develops. Is God moving you to reach the hurting in your context? Go ahead and start something. Keep asking how the fullness of God's gifts could come to bear on the broken and forgotten. Is God showing you a community that needs a church? Go ahead and start it. Begin with some core families or individuals in the area. Start serving the community. Be the presence of the Savior in that place.

Remember, your whole community is under God's umbrella of care and concern. He's given you the authority to go and make disciples.

Stoke

So, you're sharing life in Jesus with new people, you're searching for new leaders, and you're starting new churches and ministries. How can you keep multiplication momentum going? You know as well as I do that we all revert to inward thinking. Fatigue sets in. The clamor of the urgent sends us running away from strategic thinking and significant initiatives. Failures, fears, and the falling-off of essential resources lead us to believe that multiplication may be too hard, too risky or too time-consuming. Vision for outreach begins to seep away. Confidence in Jesus' strength begins to wane. The opposition seems much too strong. How can you keep going?

You need to stoke the fires of God's mission.

Let's face it, we're weaklings. We are frail and fallen sinners. It is not our might or power that can accomplish the life-transforming and eternity-giving mission of our Savior. It is only by His Spirit that the work can be done. That's why we need regular refueling of God's grace, His vision, and His mission. We need God's Word. We need to be refilled with His remarkable and lavish love for us. We need to be called back to the noble and holy mission of shining the light of Jesus in a dark world. Our daily routine needs to be connected constantly to the big plan God is accomplishing. At every meeting, for every gathering, and in every conversation, we need to remember God's goal. We need to be reconnected with Gospel DNA.

That's why the DNA marker in the next section of this book is of utmost importance. A Gospel movement cannot happen without Truth.

Questions for Discussion – Chapter Ten

1. A veteran servant of the church used to say, "Do something! Do something new! Do something new now!" What multiplication thoughts did you have as you read this chapter?

2. Read Matthew 9:9-13. How can you look beyond the church membership list to invite more people into the experience of walking with Jesus and serving others with His love?

3. How many "disciples" are you pouring into, forming, and equipping?

4. Talk about developing "network thinking" as a church for your region. What shifts can you make to impact a wider area with the Gospel?

5. How can the lavish love of God regularly refuel you and your church to be about Gospel multiplication?

Gospel DNA Journal:

People God has given me to encourage, influence and help grow in faith…

How I share, search, start and stoke…

Gospel DNA

DNA Marker Three: Truth

Chapter Eleven
Traditionally Aggressive

*"I am the way, and the truth, and the life. No one comes to the
Father except through me."
Jesus speaking to Thomas in John 14:6*

Traditionally Aggressive

One of my favorite descriptions of the Missouri Synod
was written in the 1958 Time magazine article I referenced earlier
in this book. The writer of the article said: "The synod's
salesmanship is traditionally aggressive. Its *Lutheran Hour* radio
program is the best known denominational broadcast on the air,
and its TV program, *This is the Life*, is the biggest-budget religious
telecast in the U.S."[60]

Did you catch the description? The writer called the
LCMS "traditionally aggressive." I love that moniker. A team of
branding consultants couldn't have thought of a better way to
portray my church body. Both words capture the essence of the
LCMS during its second church planting movement. First, it was
truly aggressive. Two churches were being planted every week.
Thousands of adult converts were confessing faith in Jesus. The
church dominated media ministry. Even though the very small
LCMS comprised just 1.4% of the U.S. population at the time, it
had been steadily gaining from 1% of the population in 1940.
Second, the LCMS was very traditional. In contrast to
denominations that sacrificed adherence to Biblical inerrancy and
that loosened up connections with foundational confessions, the
Lutheran Church–Missouri Synod stuck to its Biblical and
confessional moorings. It didn't budge.

---

[60] "The New Lutheran, 60.

The question is: can those two worlds really coexist? Can Gospel DNA be both vigorously multiplication oriented and staunchly founded on traditional truth? Does one exclude the other? Will multiplication inevitably result in weak theology and a watered down Gospel? Does adherence to the truth hinder the growth of the church? Is it possible for a Gospel movement to flourish when Scriptural truth is non-negotiable?

Church planting movement expert David Garrison observed something that would shock people who believe truth and growth are not compatible partners. In every church planting movement he studied, the authority of God's Word was always an essential element. Garrison commented:

> As Church Planting Movements produce multiple reproducing churches, what keeps the movement from fragmenting into a thousand heresies like a crack splintering across a car windshield? There can be only one answer: the authority of God's word. Like an invisible spinal cord aligning and supporting the movement, there runs through each Church Planting Movement a commitment to the authority of the Bible.[61]

"Like an invisible spinal cord." Truth is not only present, it is the "spinal cord," the nerve center, the reference point, that which powers and propels the movement forward. Garrison added:

> Those who have successfully navigated a Church Planting Movement are unanimous in their conviction that "it must be God's word that is authoritative for the new believers and the emerging church, not the wisdom of the missionary nor some foreign creed nor even the local church authorities." By continually pointing back to the source of one's own authority, the church planter is modeling the proper pattern for the new

---

[61] Garrison, *Church Planting Movements*, Kindle Locations 2783-2786.

believers who will soon become the new conveyers of the movement.[62]

In other words, Gospel movements do not flourish in spite of the truth; they flourish because of the truth.

Sometimes we get suspicious about the growth of the church. If a large number of people are coming to faith in Christ, if a local church is growing, if a network is planting church after church, if new leaders are being developed from a variety of backgrounds and languages, we start to wonder if something isn't right. We might wonder: Is the truth really being proclaimed? Are they compromising the Gospel? Are they using gimmicks? Having witnessed enough church "scams" in our lifetime, it can be wise to harbor some healthy suspicion. But suspicion can very well become unhealthy. If you begin to believe that the Gospel cannot create a phenomenon of rapid multiplication and that the truth can only prevail in environments that do not show increase, you fall into a trap of doubting and, perhaps, rejecting the Scriptural witness about the power and authority of the Gospel. Jesus said that while some seeds of the Word are taken away by the evil one and while others are choked out by trouble and worry, the seed of the Word also "bears fruit and yields, in one case a hundredfold, in another sixty, and in another thirty" (Matthew 13:23). God's Word does not return empty, but accomplishes God's intended purpose (Isaiah 55:11). We need to give God's Word the benefit of the doubt. We need to trust that the gates of hell cannot prevail against the advance of the Lord's Church (Matthew 16:18). We need to recognize that the Gospel is able to produce results we can't anticipate. If we confess the truth, we need to gratefully receive what the truth accomplishes.

The Truth Matters

In his book, *Surprising Insights from the Unchurched*, Thom Rainer noted how important Biblical truth is to the unchurched. He highlighted a pervasive myth: "Myth #6: We must

---

[62] Garrison, *Church Planting Movements*, Kindle Locations 2803-2806.

be careful in our teaching and preaching so that we do not communicate deep and complex Biblical truths that will confuse the unchurched." Data shows this to be untrue. "One important lesson we learned from the formerly unchurched is that we should never dilute biblical teachings for the sake of the unchurched," Rainer said. "When we asked if doctrine, or beliefs, of the church they eventually joined was important, the responses were surprising and overwhelming. Ninety-one percent of the formerly unchurched indicated that doctrine was an important factor that attracted them to the church. Perhaps equally surprising was the fact that the unchurched were more concerned about doctrine than Christians who had transferred from another church."[63]

The truth works in people's hearts and lives. The truth powers movements of the Gospel. Jesus said it best, "I am the way, and the truth, and the life" (John 14:6). Jesus IS the truth. What are the implications of His statement? Jesus embodies truth. His life is truth—His teaching, His reaching, His healing, His self-sacrificial death, His miraculous resurrection, and His Great Commission. The body of God's truth is embodied in the incarnate, crucified, risen and ascended Son of God. This earth-shaking, faith-creating, and life-transforming truth appeals to people. Jesus draws people to Himself. The Spirit creates in people a craving for what God gives. When people receive this precious gift, they cannot help but speak of what they have seen and heard (Acts 4:20).

God's Word really works and the fullness of God's truth matters to people. If the formerly unchurched overwhelmingly testify to the importance of doctrinal integrity and Scriptural soundness, leaders in the church need to give God's Word credit and trust that the Gospel is a remarkable gift that can sweep through people's hearts, transform communities, and turn the world upside down. In fact, anything other than the truth is temporary and fleeting at best, and deceptive and destructive at worst.

---

[63] Rainer, *Surprising Insights*, 45.

The Biblical balance is that "traditional" and "aggressive" always go hand-in-hand as the Gospel moves through history and people's lives. Without solid Biblical truth there would be no Gospel movements. There is power in the Good News that "God so loved the world, that he gave his only Son, that whoever believes in him should not perish but have eternal life" (John 3:16). It is revolutionary to come to the understanding that we, who were once dead in trespasses and sins, have now been made alive together with Christ by grace alone and not by works—and that God created us in Christ Jesus to do the good works He prepared in advance for us to do (Ephesians 2).

There may be times when our own familiarity with God's Word can make us forget about its revolutionary power. We may forget that the Gospel really works and that when people hear it, it may completely change their lives. It could be that a danger of becoming church professionals or regular practioners of the Word of truth is that our hearts become hard and our outlooks become skeptical. How could the truth—seemingly dry doctrinal constructs and theological propositions—work miracles and sweep through communities, transforming ordinary and unschooled people into vocal believers and evangelists? Perhaps we need to remember that it has happened before (Acts 4:13). Perhaps we need to remember that truth is not simply knowledge (John 1:14). Perhaps we need to remember the truth about the truth.

Questions for Discussion – Chapter Eleven

1. How did this chapter shed new light on the truth?

2. How do both "traditional" and "aggressive" show themselves in your life and in your church?

3. What pitfalls do you need to be aware of as you become accustomed to and familiar with the Word of God?

4. Read Matthew 13:18-23. Talk about what each obstacle to God's Word means in your life and in your church. Discuss what verse 23 means for individuals and churches.

5. Jesus said He is the Truth (John 14:6). Share a story about how God's beautiful Truth has changed someone's life (perhaps yours!).

Gospel DNA Journal:

Thoughts about what it means to be "traditionally aggressive"…

What I am thankful for in God's Word of truth…

The Truth About the Truth

*"So Jesus said to the Jews who had believed him, 'If you abide
in my word, you are truly my disciples, and you will know the
truth, and the truth will set you free.'"*
Jesus in John 8:31-32

The Shadow Side of Truth

In *Ebenezer*, the 75th anniversary book of the Missouri
Synod, Professor Theodore Engelder wrote, "People must get the
idea out of their heads that the Missourians of old were violent
men, or men who, blown up with Pharisaical pride, gloried in their
isolation."[64]

Engelder made that comment because unflinching
adherence to the truth can, at times, give the impression of an
unpleasant and unfraternal demeanor. Someone who holds to the
truth can be viewed as stubborn and inflexible. Unfortunately,
alongside the staunch adherence to the Scriptures that fuels a
movement of the Gospel, there can grow a spirit of arrogance and,
yes, even meanness. In the history of the movement called
"Missouri," there were times when "Pharisaical pride" reared its
ugly head. That spirit may have been detected in the Missouri
Synod by outside groups. An 1849 missionary publication
lambasted the Synod for "their exclusiveness and their
unpardonable one-sidedness, which in many instances is the cause
why they and their church are evil spoken of and their usefulness is
materially hindered." In 1864 another Lutheran body's publication
criticized the Missouri Synod's unwillingness to unite with other

---

[64] W.H.T. Dau, Ed., *Ebenezer: Reviews of the Work of the Missouri Synod
during Three Quarters of a Century* (St. Louis: Concordia Publishing House,
1922), 118.

Lutheran denominations: "Some say that unity must precede union…Those who magnify these differences and endeavor to keep us separate are the greatest sinners in the Church." In 1918, yet another article said, "A doctrine of rigid aloofness and separatism was developed as a wall of defense. When orthodoxy becomes so strict and strait-laced and legalistic,…the cause of unity is harmed, and union and cooperation are impossible."[65]

Just or unjust, these criticisms unmask a shadow side of taking up efforts to adhere to and defend the truth. While staunchly seeking to protect and preserve the Gospel, myths about the nature of the truth may shape the actions and attitudes of the people who purport to proclaim the true Gospel. Like barnacles, these myths attach themselves and drag down healthy and effective mission progress. Like parasites, these myths drain life out of something that was beautiful and life-giving. Believing myths about the truth can render the truth ineffective and, yes, even untrue. Let's look at a few dangerous myths that lurk in the shadows of the truth.

Myth #1: The Truth is Loveless

We live in a day and age of entertainment brawls. The greater the argument on live TV, the more we love it. The louder the shouting and disagreement, the higher the ratings. The snappier the insult in a tweet, post or blog, the more likes and comments it receives. Civil discourse has waned while disrespectful diatribes have flourished. Even in the church, hard words, blindside attacks, and arrogant spirits prevail—sometimes in the name of truth.

Mean-spirited truth-proclaimers assert that the attacks are for the sake of the truth. The vitriol becomes contagious as misguided soldiers jump on the bullying bandwagon. Truth is hard, they claim. It is unforgiving. It has no room for soft-spirited compassion. Truth is rigorous and, therefore, heartless. If you can't stand the heat, get out of the kitchen. Buck up for battle. If you can't, you must not really be about the truth.

---

[65] Dau, *Ebenezer*, 110-111.

But that's a lie. It's a myth that truth is loveless. In Ephesians chapter four, the Apostle Paul urged believers to truly express truth. He said, "I therefore, a prisoner for the Lord, urge you to walk in a manner worthy of the calling to which you have been called, with all humility and gentleness, with patience, bearing with one another in love, eager to maintain the unity of the Spirit in the bond of peace" (Ephesians 4:1–3). He went on to describe the roles and purpose of Christian leaders: "And he gave the apostles, the prophets, the evangelists, the shepherds and teachers, to equip the saints for the work of ministry, for building up the body of Christ, until we all attain to the unity of the faith and of the knowledge of the Son of God, to mature manhood, to the measure of the stature of the fullness of Christ, so that we may no longer be children, tossed to and fro by the waves and carried about by every wind of doctrine, by human cunning, by craftiness in deceitful schemes. Rather, speaking the truth in love, we are to grow up in every way into him who is the head, into Christ" (Ephesians 4:11–15).

Notice that being children not only meant being tossed to and fro by every wind of doctrine. It also meant that human cunning and deceitful schemes hold sway. What was the opposite of poor doctrine, human cunning and deceitful schemes? Speaking the truth in love. That is what grows us up into Christ. The truth is intimately connected to love. If truth becomes mean, it's not fully the truth. If truth becomes divisive instead of delightful, fearful instead of fruitful, there is a problem. Some view controversy as a sign of the true church. Sometimes it is, but at other times it simply indicates you're being mean, unfaithful to Christ's calling.

It is a fact that humbly honoring the truth of God's Word caused great challenge to the church throughout the ages. The Missouri Synod established clear Scriptural positions and drew doctrinal lines. The LCMS evaluated theological questions with rigor and engaged in strong discourse about matters of faith and practice. But being committed to the truth was never a reason for poor churchmanship or bad behavior. It was not an excuse for offensiveness or lovelessness. In *Ebenezer*, Theodore Engelder commented,

> Let no one become dismayed at the criticism that the Missouri fathers were a stern, unloving set of fighters, who forgot the gentler aspects of Christianity over their devotion to rigorous discipline, for though they minced no words when they spoke on any issue of the day, they spoke the truth, and they spoke it in love. We shall take up their testimony and pass it on. It is possible, perhaps, to present it occasionally in a more pleasing form than it was rendered in the controversial stress and storm of the past, and if we can, we ought to do so, and prove ourselves as our fathers strove to be, truth-loving and truth-telling Christian gentlemen.[66]

If truth is torn away from love, the truth is lost.

Myth #2: The Truth is Limiting

A second myth about truth is that it is limiting. Sometimes, in the struggle for pure doctrine, truth supporters add safeguards to the truth, tools and boundary markers that help keep people away from error and unfaithfulness. Every generation adds traditions, preferences, and practices that help preserve and express the truth. Unfortunately, those additions and boundary markers can begin to dominate the underlying message and spirit of the Gospel. The Pharisaical laws are a classic example of tradition trumping truth. Soon, legalism takes hold and freedom in the Gospel is lost.

The fact is, truth cannot be put in a box. Yes, the teachings of the Scriptures are non-negotiable. The Word endures forever. But Jesus is the Way and the Truth and the Life. He said in John 8, "If you abide in my word, you are truly my disciples, and you will know the truth, and the truth will set you free" (John 8:31–32). The truth expands the possibilities. God's imagination is infinite. What can be accomplished by abiding in Jesus' Word is beyond all we could ever ask for or imagine. The truth is not

---

[66] Dau, *Ebenezer*, 535-536.

constraining. It is freeing. It is limitless. The reason Christ's Church has flourished throughout the centuries is because the eternal truth has no boundaries and needs no additives. The moment we say, "Impossible," God says, "Possible." The Truth was born of a virgin. The Truth was baptized and tempted in our stead. The Truth turned water into wine at a wedding. The Truth approached lepers, hung out with tax collectors and prostitutes, walked on the water and raised the dead. The Truth washed the disciples' feet even though the disciples objected because that wasn't a fitting task for the Truth. The Truth was mocked, beaten and killed publicly—humiliated by being hung on a cross and becoming sin in our place. The Truth rose from the dead and sent ordinary people to effect eternity. The truth is not limiting. It is mind-blowing, expansive and awe-inspiring. It is reason for rejoicing.

Jesus emphasized that. He said, "If you keep my commandments, you will abide in my love, just as I have kept my Father's commandments and abide in his love. These things I have spoken to you, that my joy may be in you, and that your joy may be full" (John 15:10–11). Keeping Jesus' commandments meant abiding in His love. Abiding in His love meant that our joy would be full. Truth is not a dour and sour-spirited proposition. It is freeing and joyful. It grants permission and sends. Truth is limitless. That's why Gospel movements move like wildfire. The Gospel DNA of truth sets them loose to overtake life after life with the integrity of God's unchanging message applied in ways and by people we would never expect.

Myth #3: The Truth is Learning

One of the most common myths about the truth is that truth is simply learning, a set of facts, a body of teaching to master, memorize and muse about. This myth makes knowledge the goal. If a person has the right answers, he or she is orthodox. If they can check the right boxes and utter the proper phrases, they're members in good standing. But the Bible paints a much different picture. The truth of God's Word is never something simply to think about or debate about. Knowing a set of answers does not make a disciple. The truth is a gift from God that activates a life of faith and discipleship. James 1:22 declares, "Do not merely listen to the word, and so deceive yourselves. Do what it says" (James 1:22 NIV). Listening only, accumulating knowledge and studying until you master every syllable of God's Word, can lead to self-deception if you're not doing what the Word says. The Apostle John said it this way: "Little children, let us not love in word or talk but in deed and in truth" (1 John 3:18).

Gospel DNA doesn't just think about the Good News of salvation in Jesus Christ. Gospel DNA doesn't merely talk about God's miraculous rescue through His one and only Son. Gospel DNA doesn't simply discuss prayer, the fruits of the Holy Spirit, evangelistic outreach, stewardship, self-sacrifice, and service to others in Jesus' name. It does it. The Gospel DNA marker of truth consists in hearing the Word and doing what it says. Inactive truth is ignored truth—even if we claim to be all about the truth. Referring to false prophets, people who claimed to serve God but were ravenous wolves in sheep's clothing, Jesus said, "You will recognize them by their fruits" (Matthew 7:16). The truth is not only learning; it is also living.

At the twenty-fifth anniversary of the founding of the LCMS in 1872, President C.F.W. Walther preached a sermon that spelled out the balance of knowing the Word and doing the Word. He said:

> Yet now I seem to hear all our enemies say sneeringly: "Yes, yes, 'Reine Lehre,' 'pure doctrine,' 'orthodoxy,' –that's it, and that's about all you glory in. Vainglory!" …For what is "reine Lehre"? Pure doctrine is the pure Word of God, the pure bread of life eternal, the pure seed of the children of the Kingdom, a pure fountain of faith and love, a pure well of divine comfort, in a word, it is the clean, sure, and straight way to Christ and into heaven. Truly pure doctrine, then, is more precious than silver and gold, sweeter than honey and the honeycomb, stronger than sin, death, devil, and hell, more than heaven and earth. And

pure doctrine is never an idle or dead thing: from it, and from it alone, flows spiritual, Christian, divine life…Wherever there is purity of doctrine, there will be found miracles of divine grace, according to the promise: "The Word that proceedeth out of My mouth shall not return unto Me void, but shall accomplish that which I please, and shall prosper in the thing whereto I sent it."[67]

The truth is never "an idle or dead thing." From it "flows spiritual, Christian, divine life." We must never drift into a one-sided and unhealthy adherence to the truth. We can't fall victim to the myths. The truth will cause distinctions, but the truth is not mean and divisive. The truth will shape our action, but it will never be a slave to our preferences. The truth will always need rigorous study and committed learning, but it will never be diminished to become simply an expression of our theological intelligence.

We are called not merely to protect and preserve the truth, but to promote the truth. We steward the truth well and faithfully when we let it do its work for the Glory of God and for the salvation of His people. In the 100th Anniversary book of the Lutheran Church–Missouri Synod, Dr. Walter A. Baepler reinforced the LCMS's DNA of truth and offered two challenges for the next hundred years. He said:

The centennial of Synod calls upon its members to examine their attitude toward faithful adherence to the Word of God and to the Confessions of the Lutheran Church…The centennial of Synod must stimulate its members to reconsecrate themselves to the work of the Lord. By the grace of God the Missouri Synod has the message of justification by faith in Jesus, the message of salvation solely in the blood of the crucified Savior. The Lord, who has preserved unto this body the purity of the teachings of His Word, certainly has done this for a specific purpose, namely, that it preach the Gospel in its truth and purity

---

[67] Dau, *Ebenezer*, 312.

to a sin-stricken world...If the Missouri Synod, bountifully equipped with spiritual and material resources, refuses to discharge its obligations as a missionary agency, the Lord can and will call forth a Church to do His bidding, for "this Gospel of the Kingdom shall be preached in all the world for a witness unto all nations; and then the end shall come." Matt. 24:14.[68]

The truth is truth in action. That is what Gospel movements in the United States like the "missionary agency" of the LCMS learned as they searched for their identity in a new nation and as they struggled to move forward during changing times. When followers of Jesus really abide in Him, when they are truly attentive to His Word, the truth sets them free to accomplish God's remarkable life-bestowing mission. But what does it take to abide in Jesus? Moving the truth out of the shadows always requires a healthy dose of humility.

---

[68] Baepler, *A Century of Grace*, 357-358.

Questions for Discussion – Chapter Twelve

1. What thoughts did you have as you read about the shadow side of the truth?

2. What does it mean to speak the truth in love—in your personal relationships and as a church?

3. If truth is meant to be promoted as well as preserved, what hopes and dreams do you have for reaching people with the Gospel? Take time to stretch your imagination about how people you love, your community, and the world might be reached through your Gospel efforts.

4. Read James 1:22 and 1 John 3:18. How is the truth of salvation by grace through faith in Jesus Christ showing itself in your action toward others?

5. How might the myths mentioned in this chapter get in the way of sharing the truth of Jesus with the people you love the most?

Gospel DNA Journal:

How I veer into the myths about the truth…

What helps balance both the preservation and promotion of the truth…

Chapter Thirteen
Truth and Humility

"If we say we have no sin, we deceive ourselves, and the truth is not in us."
The Apostle John in 1 John 1:8

Whose Baby?

A joyful and fulfilling part of my ministry was having the chance to help "restart" a mission church in the northwest suburbs of Chicago. The dedicated and caring band of believers there taught me what it meant to be the church. They showed Jesus' love; they served the community and one another; they shared the Gospel; they gave glory to God in all they did. A telling indicator of the spirit of this little church was the two statements they included in their information packet to me about the church's purpose. As I considered their invitation to join them in mission, I read these two concise statements printed in capital letters:

TO REACH OUT INTO THE COMMUNITY WITH GOD'S WORD.
TO REACH OUT INTO THE COMMUNITY WITH GOD'S ACTION.

I was convinced. I had to be a part of this mission. These were people who understood the truth. God's great gift of new life in Jesus Christ was an exciting adventure. They wanted to lean into it with joy and gusto. So my wife and I packed up our possessions, piled into our car with our nine-month-old daughter, and made the trip from Minnesota to our new mission field. We served there for fifteen years. And what a wonderful fifteen years it was. The people not only backed up their statements with action, they invited and welcomed many others to join them in this mission. The ranks of missionaries swelled—young and old. Many people received the blessing of new life in Christ. Ministry there was full of miraculous and beautiful surprises. But one surprise caught me off guard: my own attitude.

As the years went by and as I became more invested in the people of the church, in the community, and in our mission, I started to feel like this vibrant mission church was my "child." I tried not to become possessive of this ministry—I was God's steward, not the owner—but some of my reactions to situations began to signal an overprotective spirit and a tendency toward control. I didn't like it. I knew it wasn't healthy. This church was not my baby. It was God's. The possessiveness and arrogance creeping into my heart was not healthy. I knew it could hinder the church's mission.

As followers of Christ, possessiveness and arrogance can creep into our hearts as we work with His Word of truth. We become familiar with God's Word. We see it having a remarkable and transformational impact on people's lives. We memorize Bible verses and talk about Biblical principles. We handle the Word of truth frequently and regularly. But there is a danger. As fallen and sinful "know-it-alls," we can begin to believe that God's Word is "our baby."

You may have been in this unholy place. You start to take pride in your clever and skilled communication as the best way for people to really understand God's Word. You begin to believe that the setting you provide for worship and study is the best way—and, perhaps, the only right way—for people to be in the presence of the truth effectively. You have a sense that if the rest of the Christian Church listened to you and learned from you, the church would be much better off. You feel like most everyone else in the Holy Christian Church is off the mark; they're doing it all wrong; they need to change.

The Apostle Paul said to young Timothy, "Do your best to present yourself to God as one approved, a worker who has no need to be ashamed, rightly handling the word of truth" (2 Timothy 2:15). Paul urged Timothy to avoid empty talk and a spirit that would throw him off the path of God being his close companion and leader. Paul didn't want Timothy to veer into godlessness, supplanting God's Word with his own words, arguments and pride. We do well to listen to Paul's counsel. Acting like we own God's message sends us on a pathway away from the truth. And it harms God's mission.

Truth and Humility

Psalm 2 has advice for all of us who are tempted to believe that God's Kingdom is our kingdom, that we're the ones running the show with full understanding: "Now therefore, O kings, be wise; be warned, O rulers of the earth. Serve the Lord with fear, and rejoice with trembling" (Psalms 2:10–11).

Fear and trembling. The antidote to arrogance and pride is fear and trembling, humility and repentance. There is no doubt, we like to be right. But even if we're completely right about something, there is always something wrong in us. The Apostle John urged people to walk in truth by remaining in Christ. He said, "If we say we have no sin, we deceive ourselves, and the truth is not in us" (1 John 1:8). If we get into the dangerous position of claiming to be completely right, we live in deception and deny the truth. This does not mean that truth is relative and that we have to be wishy-washy about God's Word. This isn't an attempt to create a doctrinal free-for-all in the church. It means that, as we stand firmly on God's infallible and inerrant Word, we stand humbly and with a spirit of repentance. We never claim to have no sin, no blind spots, and no need to learn and to grow in understanding. Handling the Word of truth properly means handling it as beggars who have been given the precious bread of life. The Gospel DNA marker of truth advances Gospel movements when truth is spoken in love by grateful servants of God who understand that "God chose what is low and despised in the world, even things that are not, to bring to nothing things that are, so that no human being might boast in the presence of God" (1 Corinthians 1:28–29).

Dr. Rosaria Butterfield discovered this firsthand. Rosaria was a highly qualified and popular English professor at Syracuse University. She said, "At the age of 36, I was one of the few tenured women at a large research university, a rising administrator, and a community activist. I had become one of the 'tenured radicals.'"[69] Just eight years earlier, she announced that she was a lesbian. She was also an atheist. She was interested in matters of faith, but only intellectually. Rosaria believed that her talents, ideologies, and trajectory in life were making the world a better place. Then came what she describes as the "train wreck" of coming face-to-face with the living God. It all started by having dinner with Pastor Ken Smith and his wife Floy. Ken pastored the little Reformed Presbyterian church in town. He read a column Rosaria wrote in the local newspaper lambasting Promise Keepers, a Christian men's movement that happened to be holding a rally in town. Ken wrote to Rosaria inviting her to dinner and discussion with him and his wife. Rosaria accepted the invitation. She reflected on their first encounter:

> Ken and Floy did something at the meal that has a long Christian history but has been functionally lost in too many Christian homes. Ken and Floy invited the stranger in— not to scapegoat me, but to listen and to learn and to dialogue. Ken and Floy have a vulnerable and transparent faith. We didn't debate worldview; we talked about our personal truth and about what "made us tick." Ken and Floy didn't identify with me. They listened to me and identified with Christ. They were willing to walk the long journey to me in Christian compassion. During our meal, they did not share the gospel with me. After our meal, they did not invite me to church. Because of these glaring omissions to the Christian script as I had come to know it, when the evening ended and Pastor Ken said he wanted to stay in touch, I knew that it was truly safe to accept his open hand.[70]

---

[69] Rosaria Champagne Butterfield, *The Secret Thoughts of an Unlikely Convert: Expanded Edition* (Crown & Covenant Publications, 2014), Kindle Edition, Kindle Locations 80-82.
[70] Rosaria Butterfield, *The Secret Thoughts*, Kindle Locations 305-311.

The truth was being spoken and lived in love. Rosaria commented about how she saw the truth accompanied by respect, kindness and self-sacrifice:

> I wanted to get to know these people but not at the expense of compromising my moral standards. My lesbian identity and culture and its values mattered a lot to me. I came to my culture and its values through life experience but also through much research and deep thinking. I liked Ken and Floy immediately because they seemed sensitive to that. Even though obviously these Christians and I were very different, they seemed to know that I wasn't just a blank slate, that I had values and opinions too, and they talked with me in a way that didn't make me feel erased.[71]

Rosaria Butterfield expressed very perceptively that the DNA marker of truth—though jarring, confronting, and exposing, while at the same time being comforting, constructing and encouraging—advances God's mission by being spoken in love. She said, "Good teachers make it possible for people to change their positions without shame."[72] That's what Pastor Ken Smith did. Rosaria reflected:

> Before I ever set foot in a church, I spent two years meeting with Ken and Floy and on and off "studying" Scripture and my heart. If Ken and Floy had invited me to church at that first meal I would have careened like a skateboard off a cliff, and would have never come back. Ken, of course, knows the power of the word preached but it seemed to me he also knew at that time that I couldn't come to church— it would have been too threatening, too weird, too much. So, Ken was willing to bring the church to me.[73]

---

[71] Butterfield, *The Secret Thoughts*, Kindle Locations 287-291.
[72] Butterfield, *The Secret Thoughts*, Kindle Locations 369-370.
[73] Butterfield, *The Secret Thoughts*, Kindle Locations 316-320.

Humbly, gently, respectfully, Ken Smith met Rosaria Butterfield where she was. He wasn't afraid God's Word would come crumbling down because he was meeting with her. He didn't think God couldn't handle her questions or objections. He had no illusion that he was in charge of this remarkable new friendship. He simply held out the Word of life as "a lamp shining in a dark place," until the day dawned and the morning star rose in her heart (2 Peter 1:19). The Holy Spirit was doing something beautiful through two broken people.

Rosaria understood that the truth—solid, sound and miraculous Biblical truth— brought her the gift of faith in Jesus Christ and transformed her life now and forever. I highly recommend that you read the book for the details of her story and for insights about the church reaching the culture today. Rosaria Butterfield summed up the interplay of truth expressed in love with humility: "Biblical orthodoxy can offer real compassion, because in our struggle against sin we cannot undermine God's power to change lives."[74]

Gospel movements happen not because we're right about everything and not because we're in charge. They happen because God's Word is living and active, powerful and grace-filled. We humbly bow before our Savior and handle the truth as servants. Over and over again we return to our gracious and faithful God by His grace and by the power of the Holy Spirit to be entrusted with His mysteries that penetrate the hearts and souls of the people He dearly loves. You and I will never be at the center of the movement of the Gospel. We will never be the authorities, the gurus, or the experts. We will never be "more righteous" than people who are not in our camp. Jesus is the One at the center. He humbles. He equips. He sends. Sometimes His ways are completely unpredictable. My denomination had to learn that lesson as God showed them that truth without mission was only half the truth.

---

[74] Butterfield, *The Secret Thoughts*, Kindle Locations 552-553.

Questions for Discussion – Chapter Thirteen

1. What caught your attention most in this chapter?

2. How might you tend to make the Gospel and the church "your baby"?

3. Talk about the balance of humility and truth in the contexts of dealing with fellow Christians and with people who do not have faith in Christ.

4. Read Hebrews 13:1-2. Welcoming the stranger is something Dr. Rosaria Butterfield recommends highly in our disconnected culture—especially as a way to build relationships and share what is most important in our lives. In what ways does your church welcome the stranger, and how can that practice can grow and develop?

5. How did the Gospel DNA markers of love and care for people, multiplication and truth play out in the relationship between Ken Smith and Rosaria Butterfield? How can you apply this to the way you connect with people for Jesus?

Gospel DNA Journal:

What it looks like to serve the Lord with fear, and rejoice with trembling …

Whom God is allowing me to be a source of truth to…

Truth and Mission

"For this purpose I was born and for this purpose I have come into the world—to bear witness to the truth. Everyone who is of the truth listens to my voice."
Jesus answering Pontius Pilate in John 18:37

Bearing Witness to the Truth

Jesus came, as He said very clearly, to bear witness to the truth (John 18:37). He emphasized that whoever listens to His voice is of the truth. Jesus connected truth with His mission to seek and to save the lost. Truth and mission are bound together. But we don't always reflect that fact in our intentions or actions. The forefathers of my church body did not come to the United States to bear witness to the truth. The Saxons came to the United States seeking protection from European church leaders who were forcing Lutherans to mingle Reformed doctrine with their teaching. To be honest, outreach with the Gospel was not the primary concern of Stephan's band of immigrants. In his book, *Teach My People the Truth*, Herman Zehnder noted: "They had not come to America for a missionary purpose. They had fled Saxony because they were dissatisfied with the doctrinal conditions of the Lutheran Church in Saxony. Their overriding concern was to preserve for themselves and their descendants purity of doctrine and adherence to the Lutheran Confessions."[75]

Historian Walter Forster also emphasized that preserving the truth was the primary concern of Lutherans in America. The goal was noble and the people were zealous about taking their stand. But after the collapse of the Stephan experiment, the

---

[75] Herman Zehnder, *Teach My People the Truth* (Frankenmuth, Michigan: Herman Zehnder, 1970), 86.

Lutheran group from Saxony began to receive harsh criticism from the homeland. They were accused of not being the true church. They didn't have bishops like the church in Europe. There was no sanctioning authority like the old world ecclesiastical powers. They were even told that they didn't have a liturgy. An identity crisis gripped the new immigrants. Were they or weren't they the church? Could they be the church without institutional sanction? Was their presence valid in the new land? C.F.W. Walther joined his Saxon counterparts in wrestling over these issues. Walther sought answers in the Scriptures, the Confessions, and in Martin Luther's writings. He came away from his study and deliberation with a new outlook. First, the Saxons did constitute the church. Walther said, "The name of the true Church belongs also to all those visible companies of men among whom God's Word is purely taught and the holy Sacraments are administered according to the institution of Christ."[76] Second, convicted by the exclusive and oppressive spirit of Martin Stephan, Walther and his companions were brought to heart-rending repentance. They began to realize that the Saxons had a new task in the United States. They needed to reach out. They needed to make an effort to unite people around the truth of the Scriptures and Lutheran Confessions and they needed to reach a growing nation with the truth of the Gospel. The first constitution of the LCMS reflected this balanced emphasis. Written chiefly by Walther, the sixth and final point in the first article, stating reasons for the organization of the synod, said: "United effort to extend the kingdom of God and to make possible the promotion of special church projects." One of the projects noted in parentheses was "mission work within and outside the church."[77] Mission was being reunited with truth. The LCMS was beginning its journey to become "traditionally aggressive."

---

[76] Forster, *Zion*, 524.

[77] W.G. Polack, *How the Missouri Synod was Born* (Chicago: Walther League, 1947), 37.

As the decades passed and hundreds of thousands of people had been reached with the Gospel, the truth of the Scriptures and Confessions were seen as a strength—not just strength in thought and theological position, but in mission. In 1919 John H.C. Fritz said, "In the exclusive doctrinal position of our Lutheran Church is not only to be found its strength, but therein also lies its great missionary possibility."[78]

Facing the materialism, skepticism, and rationalism of a nation by holding up flimsy theology and doubt-filled doctrinal constructs was no way to bring the life-transforming Gospel to sinners in need of God's salvation. The truth, the authority of God's Word, the clear and unequivocal teaching of Jesus Christ as Savior—crucified and risen—is what changed people's lives and formed the church. There was no compromise—not because of a stubborn or contentious spirit, but because of "missionary possibility." L. Meyer captured this spirit in his 1937 publication, *Torch Bearers*:

> The Missouri Synod today stands equipped spiritually, morally, and physically as no other church body in the world to carry out the command of the Savior to go and preach the Gospel to the whole world. We have received from God, as an inheritance through our forefathers, *orthodoxy*. But do we always all realize the implications and obligations of the fact that we have the pure Gospel?[79]

> We must continue to work in the wilderness of this world, speaking with that voice which alone has authority in our day of sneering skepticism and rampant materialism. And we need not be afraid. We can go about our task with a song in our hearts. Christ is unchanged. His power is the same today that it was yesterday and forever will be. He is not bound by any fetters of modern forging, and because of His power and the power with

---

[78] Fritz, *The Practical Missionary*, 11.
[79] Meyer, *Torch Bearers*, 14.

which He invests His Word the wonder of conversion still remains.[80]

This connection of truth and mission was not only found in LCMS centennial booklets and in the exhortations of a few outreach minded people in the synod. It was embedded in the fabric of the denomination. It was the Gospel DNA of truth coursing through the veins of the church. It was even taught at the seminary.

Textbook Truth

In 1920, Dr. John H.C. Fritz became the dean of Concordia Seminary in St. Louis after serving twenty-three years in parish ministry. While at the seminary, he wrote the book, *Pastoral Theology*, a practical guide for seminary students as they prepared to enter pastoral ministry. The book wasn't all new. It was an update of C.F.W. Walther's Pastoral Theology, providing an English language tool for future pastors and making new ministry applications for a new generation. Fritz's book was published in 1932. I have the copy my pastor used in his seminary classes in the 1940s. This was the textbook for pastors. It outlined practical pastoral practice in a variety of areas like personal health, the pastor and the priesthood of all believers, the call to ministry, beginning a pastorate, preaching, worship, pastoral care, and church administration. It also addressed the way God's truth moves into new lives. Fritz taught pastors about the truth in action.

The book contains instructions about how to plant a new church by canvassing a neighborhood, following up on prospects, and engaging the laypeople in the church planting task. Church planting at a local level was normal for LCMS congregations. It was textbook truth.

Fritz urged pastors to engage in missionary visits, "calls" made to unchurched people. After reprimanding pastors and congregations for not growing in membership through outreach to the unchurched, Fritz urged vibrant missionary and church-planting

---

[80] Meyer, *Torch Bearers*, 32-33.

action: "It is surprising how few calls some pastors and missionaries make; and it is equally surprising how many others, deeply interested in the saving of souls, can make. One of our pastors writes: 'Besides being janitor, sign-card writer, etc., for my mission, I have in five months made 1,014 missionary calls.'"[81] That's almost seven connections with new people each day for five months! Truth was coupled with bold action.

And who was being reached? Fritz said: "The question whether or not work in the new field should be undertaken should not be determined by the number of stray Lutherans that might be found there or by the number of people speaking a certain language or belonging to a particular class (rich or poor) or by the number of prospects, but by the fact that there are unchurched people living in that territory."[82]

This was the teaching seminary students received. The truth was not to be hidden away in order to protect it. The truth was not to be withheld from people who didn't seem to "fit" a certain niche or class. The truth was not to be kept in the classroom or study or church building. The truth was for sharing, promoting and proclaiming to all people. The fullness of the truth is ultimately expressed in mission. And as we fix our eyes on Jesus, we hear His call to "Go into all the world and proclaim the Gospel to the whole creation" (Mark 16:15). How, then, can you walk in the truth with maximum mission purpose?

---

[81] Fritz, *Pastoral Theology*, 289.
[82] Fritz, *Pastoral Theology*, 295-296.

Questions for Discussion – Chapter Fourteen

1. What about the relationship of truth and mission in this chapter stretched your thinking?

2. John H.C. Fritz said in 1919: "In the exclusive doctrinal position of our Lutheran Church is not only to be found its strength, but therein also lies its great missionary possibility." What does this statement mean for you, for your church, and for the Christian Church in the world?

3. What are "the implications and obligations" of having the pure Gospel?

4. John H.C. Fritz mentioned people who were "deeply interested in the saving of souls." What can help develop that deep interest in you and in your church?

5. What unreached group of people exists in your community? How can you begin reaching them with the Gospel?

Gospel DNA Journal:

The people I really have a heart for are …

What a "missionary call" looks like in my life…

Chapter Fifteen

How to Walk in Truth

"Sanctify them in the truth; your word is truth."
Jesus praying for His disciples in John 17:17

To Whom Shall We Go?

In John chapter 6, Jesus spoke truth that tested every listener. He said, "Whoever feeds on my flesh and drinks my blood has eternal life, and I will raise him up on the last day" (vs. 54). As He taught in the synagogue in Capernaum, Jesus kept pushing the point: "Whoever feeds on this bread will live forever" (vs. 58). His listeners reacted strongly: "When many of his disciples heard it, they said, 'This is a hard saying; who can listen to it?'" (vs. 60) Finally, people bailed on Jesus. John reports, "After this many of his disciples turned back and no longer walked with him" (vs. 66).

They didn't want to hear the truth anymore. It became too demanding, too overwhelming, too much beyond what they could imagine and what they wanted to pursue. So Jesus turned to the Twelve and asked, "Do you want to go away as well?" Peter spoke up: "Lord, to whom shall we go? You have the words of eternal life, and we have believed, and have come to know, that you are the Holy One of God" (vss. 67–69).

Peter knew he had no other option. If he left Jesus, he would be living under his own failing power and frail insight. If he stuck around, he may feel confused and at risk, but he would remain connected to the One who had the words of eternal life, the Holy One of God. He couldn't leave. He would walk the hard road of truth.

What about you? On one hand, you may feel safe and secure by drifting into isolation because of fear. If you shut the world out and keep learning pure doctrine, at least you can teach classes with reliable content, preach some sound sermons, and steer believers into correct teaching. But what about Jesus' bold call to go into all the world and make disciples? What about Jesus' invitation to deny yourself, take up your cross and follow Him?

On the other hand, you may be charging out into the world, ready to take another hill for the Kingdom, but Biblical teaching feels like it's slowing you down. Your gut is telling you that it would be much easier to take some shortcuts and disconnect from the parts of Scripture that hamper your mission. You may feel like it's time to update God's Word so you can accelerate the pace of your plan. But what about Jesus' prayer to be sanctified in the Word of truth?

Today Peter calls out to you and me, "To whom shall we go?" If you hide in your safe cocoon, you walk away from hard teaching and get lost in the personal enjoyment of knowledge. If you cut yourself loose from God's Word, you nudge Jesus aside and leave Him behind. Remember, Peter tried that. When he insisted that Jesus should not fulfill the divine plan of suffering and death, Jesus rebuked him by saying, "Get behind me, Satan! You are a hindrance to me. For you are not setting your mind on the things of God, but on the things of man" (Matthew 16:23).

How can you walk in truth? How can you keep in mind the things of God in your life as His follower and servant? How can the balanced and beautiful Gospel DNA marker of truth abide in your life?

Walking in Prayer

The answer begins in the Way and the Truth and the Life, Jesus. In John 17, Jesus prayed for His disciples. His actions and words help us understand what it means to walk in the truth, not veering into fears or false gospels. It is absolutely remarkable to hear Jesus pray for His disciples. This was His habit. He regularly took time away to speak with his Father in heaven. Before He started His mission as Messiah by being baptized, He prayed. Before He chose the twelve, he prayed all night. Before He was transfigured on the mountaintop, He prayed. Before He went to the cross, He prayed. And as He prepared His disciples for their mission on earth, He prayed.

Prayer is the bedrock of the movement of the Gospel. When you pray, "Your Kingdom come, Your will be done," you are putting your feelings and preferences aside. You are bowing before the Holy God as His servant. You are admitting to God that this is about Him, not you. Prayer makes room for God to do His work. After Jesus ascended into heaven, the believers followed in His steps: they prayed. Acts chapter 1 tells us: "All [the disciples] with one accord were devoting themselves to prayer, together with the women and Mary the mother of Jesus, and his brothers" (Acts 1:14). These first disciples expressed complete dependence on God's plan and purpose through prayer.

I'll never forget the conversation I had with a group of young people who visited our church from the former Soviet Union. Communism had crumbled and now these twenty-somethings wanted to learn about ministry to children. They came a long way to dialog about how to reach more people with the Gospel. I asked them, "How did you even find out about Jesus when the Gospel was suppressed for so long?" One answer they gave was: "We saw our grandparents praying."

Prayer begins and undergirds Gospel movements. Prayer keeps you connected with the Truth.

When I began my ministry, I intentionally dialogued with ministry veterans, people who had served for many years and, in some cases, had retired years ago. One question I asked was, "What would you do differently if you could do it all over again?" One response was: "I would have spent more time in prayer."

These pastors knew the power of prayer—personally, for their families, for the people of God they pastored, and for the mission of God. Prayer preceded Pentecost. Prayer precedes every movement of the Gospel. Are you praying? Not teaching about prayer, studying about prayer, talking about prayer, reading about prayer, and thinking about prayer. Are you immersed in the same privilege in which the prophets, Jesus, and His disciples were immersed? Are you praying intentionally and regularly—

constantly (1 Thessalonians 5:17)? Are you lifting up God's people in prayer? Are you praying that the Lord of the harvest will send more workers? Are you praying for the lost? Are you bringing the puzzling questions of this generation to the Father in prayer? Are you waiting eagerly for His gracious response and leading?

Walking in prayer keeps you walking in truth.

Walking in the Word

Another answer those veteran pastors gave when I asked them what they would do differently was: "I would have spent more time in God's Word." This answer reflects Jesus' prayer and priority for His disciples. He said, "I have given them your word, and the world has hated them because they are not of the world, just as I am not of the world...Sanctify them in the truth; your word is truth" (John 17:14, 17). The Word of God would be their lifeblood. Without it, they would be empty. There would be no reason to be sent. There could be no movement.

Every person I've known who has served God well was a person of the Word. God's Word oozed from their pores. It seasoned their language. It formed their thinking. It shaped their worldview. It fed their faith. It gave them vision. Are you in God's Word? There is no rulebook that mandates how often you read or hear the Scriptures or how much you cover in one sitting, but the writer of Psalm 119 captured the trajectory of how we need to lean in to God's Word: "I rejoice in following your statutes as one rejoices in great riches. I meditate on your precepts and consider your ways. I delight in your decrees; I will not neglect your word" (Psalms 119:14–16 NIV). He adds, "Your testimonies are my delight; they are my counselors" (vs. 24). The entire beautiful Psalm lauds the gift of God's Word, but I'll just add one more pace-setting statement for our need to be saturated with God's Word: "Oh how I love your law! It is my meditation all the day" (vs. 97).

How are you making your way through God's Word? Read, focus and reflect. Let a verse or small section of the

Scriptures percolate in your heart and soul for a few days. Read through the great accounts of God's servants in the Old Testament. Listen to Jesus' voice in the Gospels. Walk with the Apostles as they counsel Christians in the early church. Use a devotional book to walk in the Word. Listen to podcasts. Use your study and preparation time to go in depth. However you do it, don't neglect the Word. Make it your meditation all day. Ask yourself what the text is for everything you do. Journal your thoughts, talk your reading over with a friend, pray over the Word, ponder God's message while you go out for a run or while you're driving. Heed the advice of people who have gone before. You will never regret that you've spent too much time in God's Word.

When God's Word is your constant companion, your intimate friend, you will become a person of truth. You will benchmark all you do against the Scriptures. Your preferences will never prevail over the Word of God. Those elements of life or ministry that would try to usurp authority or attention over God's Word will be left on the cutting room floor—even things you may really love. God's Word will have first priority. The DNA marker of truth will prevail in your life if you hear the Word of God and keep it (Luke 11:28).

Walking in the Spirit

As He prayed to His Father in John 17, Jesus added, "I do not ask that you take them out of the world, but that you keep them from the evil one. They are not of the world, just as I am not of the world" (John 17:15–16). This was a perceptive prayer. Jesus knew that one of the most alluring temptations we will face as His servants is to be of the world. It is tempting to imitate the world's methods and attitudes even as we handle the holy things of God. One of my favorite quotes from Henri Nouwen, renowned author and Christian thinker is, "Power offers an easy substitute for the hard task of love."[83] How easy it is for us to become people of force and coercion—even bullying—as we represent God's

---

[83] Henri Nouwen, In *the Name of Jesus: Reflections on Christian Leadership* (New York: Crossroad, 1994), 59.

precious truth. The seeds of this poisonous growth are in all of us. Ego feeds this toxic tendency: we want to be known by more people; we want to be an authority; we want to be cheered by the crowds. Impatience and selfishness add unhealthy nutrients to this destructive infestation: getting our way becomes the focus; the truth becomes an excuse for our pursuit of personal power. We need to be kept from the snares of the evil one—and we need to be guarded from our own sinful vulnerabilities.

The Apostle Paul gave us a beautiful answer to our fleshly struggle. He said, "You, however, are not in the flesh but in the Spirit, if in fact the Spirit of God dwells in you" (Romans 8:9). As we fall humbly before the Lord, Peter let us know about the certainty of the Holy Spirit in us: "Repent and be baptized every one of you in the name of Jesus Christ for the forgiveness of your sins, and you will receive the gift of the Holy Spirit. For the promise is for you and for your children and for all who are far off, everyone whom the Lord our God calls to himself" (Acts 2:38–39). As the Holy Spirit has been given to us, we are urged, "Live by the Spirit, and you will not gratify the desires of the sinful nature" (Galatians 5:16 NIV).

Paul helps us to define what living by the Spirit means. He said, "Whatever is true, whatever is honorable, whatever is just, whatever is pure, whatever is lovely, whatever is commendable, if there is any excellence, if there is anything worthy of praise, think about these things. What you have learned and received and heard and seen in me—practice these things, and the God of peace will be with you" (Philippians 4:8–9). Walking in truth involves not only content but character. We're called to practice living in the truth. Putting to death those things which discredit and dishonor the truth, we look for the fruit borne by the Spirit in our lives. The Apostle Paul noted these for us: "But the fruit of the Spirit is love, joy, peace, patience, kindness, goodness, faithfulness, gentleness, self-control" (Galatians 5:22–23). These descriptors help identify whether or not we are actually in the truth. The Apostle John emphasized, "If we say we have fellowship with him while we walk in darkness, we lie and do not practice the truth" (1 John 1:6).

This calls for personal discipline, devotion and accountability. An older pastor shared something I never forgot. Speaking about a harsh group of people trying to get their way at a gathering of the church, he said to me, "They're right, but they're being mean about it. You need to be right in the right way." Truth flourishes when we walk in the company of Jesus and in the power of the Spirit.

Walking in Discipleship

Jesus closed out His prayer for His disciples by saying, "As you sent me into the world, so I have sent them into the world. And for their sake I consecrate myself, that they also may be sanctified in truth" (John 17:18–19). These are words of sending and multiplication. Walking in the truth, as you've read in this section, means not only knowing, but doing. It not only involves protecting the truth, but promoting the truth. It is not merely saying the truth, but sending people with the truth. It is putting the Word of God to work.

Who are you pouring into in order to develop more disciples? Who are you sending to do Gospel work in their sphere of influence and relationships? Who are your "twelve disciples"? If you want to walk in the truth, you can't keep it to yourself. You can't claim to be the only available dispensary of the truth. It is against the nature and Word of the Truth Himself, Jesus Christ. Walking in the truth means active discipleship.

Early in my high school years, my pastor invited me to come with him on Sunday afternoons to visit nursing homes. I was a novice guitar player, so he asked me to play some songs for the people during the devotion time. I didn't want to do it. Play guitar in front of people? It was too scary. But I went along. I'll never forget the tears in the eyes of the men and the women who sang along to my rough accompaniment of "What a Friend We Have in Jesus." It was and is a defining moment in my life. What was my pastor doing? Did he really need me? Was it essential to have a nervous and somewhat unskilled high school sophomore along with him at his Sunday afternoon nursing home outreach? Not at all. But he was discipling me. My gifts were meant for mission, for promoting the truth of the Gospel to ones in need. He was doing the work of multiplication. That's what the truth does.

My denomination developed a system of discipleship. The LCMS established a network of schools—elementary, high schools, colleges and seminaries—for the purpose of discipleship. These Lutheran Schools were not merely places for indoctrination or for the preservation of the culture. They became centers of missionary training and sending. To this day, from early childhood centers to universities and seminaries, Lutheran schools are a treasure of discipleship—of promoting the truth. God has brought the world to LCMS classrooms—including many unchurched children, young people and adults. School classrooms are places where the love of Christ can be seen for the very first time, where the truth of the Gospel can embrace hearts that need hope, and where the calling to make Christ's difference in a broken world can be heard and followed.

The question for today is: how will we infuse active discipleship into a new culture that is drifting away from the church? How can we steward the resources we have and find new ways to share the treasure of the truth with a new generation? The answer is found in another Gospel DNA marker: Adaptability.

Questions for Discussion – Chapter Fifteen

1. How were you challenged most in this chapter?

2. Walking in prayer is not always easy, but it causes remarkable results. Talk about your prayer life and your church's prayer life. What one new prayer action can help prayer saturate your life and ministry?

3. What is your current rhythm of reading God's Word? How can God's Word be better integrated into what you say and do?

4. Read Galatians 5:22-26. How do you see yourself and the church getting out of step with the Spirit? What in these verses helps realign you with God's Spirit?

5. Discuss the questions asked in this chapter: Who are you pouring into in order to develop more disciples? Who are you sending to do Gospel work in their sphere of influence and relationships? Who are your "twelve disciples"?

Gospel DNA Journal:

I am refilled with God's wonderful truth when…

Situations when I feel like exerting power, but need to show the love God has shown me in Christ…

Gospel DNA

DNA Marker Four: Adaptability

Marker Four: Adaptability
Chapter Sixteen

Back to the Core

"With what shall I come before the Lord, and bow myself before God ön high? ...He has told you, O man, what is good; and what does the Lord require of you but to do justice, and to love kindness, and to walk humbly with your God?"
The Prophet Micah to a straying people in Micah 6:6 & 8

Adaptability vs. Creativity

When beginning to research Gospel movement characteristics around the world today and any possible indication that my denomination displayed marks of a Gospel movement in history, I initially concluded that creativity was a key DNA marker of a flourishing church. I saw new methods implemented, new technology embraced, and new ideas moving the church forward. But then I read an essay by LCMS founder, C.F.W. Walther. Written in 1862 as a reply to a critic, it was titled, "Do We Lack Creative Activity?" Walther said, "Before we can plan and undertake to become 'creatively' active, we can at present only regard it as a holy obligation first of all to learn to know, appropriate, and share the treasures of doctrine and insight which God has bestowed by His grace during the nearly 2,000 years of the church's life, and particularly 300 years ago through the work of the Lutheran reformation of the church."[84]

Three-hundred years after the Reformation, Walther directed readers back to the core truths of Christianity. Instead of thinking up new things, Walther understood and emphasized that we've been given a precious treasure. Referring to the Parable of the Talents in Matthew chapter 25, he noted that our first calling is

---

[84] Herbert J.A. Bouman, trans., Editorials *from "Lehre und Wehre"* (St. Louis: Concordia Publishing House, 1981), 106.

to be faithful servants, putting the Word to work rather than keeping what we've been given "wrapped in the napkin of our libraries." He said, "To let what has already been given the church lie unused, so that we ourselves might be 'creatively' active, could be motivated on our part by nothing but dreadful ingratitude and arrogance."[85]

Walther saw how people were substituting personal opinions and experiences for the Scriptures. He commented how in Germany during the late 1800s there seemed to be as many theologies as there were theologians. If creativity meant leaving the "old, old story" behind, he would have no part in it. But Walther did hint at a key DNA marker of a Gospel movement: adaptability. He noted: "We Missourians are conscious of no other calling than to bring forth anew the treasures of our old truly reformed church after these have long reposed uselessly as dead capital in our inherited libraries."[86] We needed "to bring forth *anew* the treasures" we've been given. If creativity means crafting new ideas—perhaps disconnected from enduring truths— adaptability means keeping original material and bringing it to bear in a new context.

Adaptability in place of creativity was reinforced by Steve Addison in his book *Movements That Change the World*. As I mentioned in chapter seven, Addison included "Adaptive Methods" as one of his five keys to spreading the Gospel. He realized that adaptability was a balancing act: honoring foundational beliefs while at the same time finding new ways to transmit those truths to new people in new contexts. Paraphrasing Jim Collins from his book *Built to Last*, Addison said, "Adaptive methods enable a movement to function in ways that suit its changing environment and its expansion into new fields. A movement's commitment to both its core ideology and to its own expansion provides the catalyst for continual learning, renewal and growth."[87]

---

[85] Bouman, *Editorials*, 106.

[86] Bouman, *Editorials*, 111-112.

[87] Addison, *Movements*, 104-105.

The Balance

After Walther put me in my place regarding creativity, I had to change my vocabulary and adjust my thinking. He was right. It wasn't creativity that marked the rapid expansion of the Missouri Synod; it was adaptability. Addison's comments reinforced my adjustment. A Gospel movement happens when followers of Christ value the truths of Christianity so much that they become determined to pass those truths along to everyone possible—usually starting with a people group or population segment to which they have natural access. Adaptability means balance. As Addison said, "Christianity's stubborn intransigence combined with flexibility in methods was a key to its success."[88]

The word "stubborn" fits the German-rooted denomination I know so well, but so does the phrase "flexibility in methods"—as we'll see in chapter nineteen. My denomination did not want to sacrifice the truth. It was—and is—tenacious about guarding it. There would be absolutely no change in the Biblical and confessional foundations of the church. Yet, its methods would be adjusted for the purpose of the Gospel. Even the act of forming a denomination in a new nation showed adaptability for the sake of the Gospel.

But this is where fear can easily raise its ugly head. "Change" is a word that strikes terror in the hearts of many. I've heard it said that once you do something for the first time, it becomes a tradition. I saw this in our own children. If mom was away and I tried to implement dad's methods at mealtime, bath time, or bed time, I would hear consistently, "But mom doesn't do it that way!" Even toddlers don't like change. Human beings are creatures of habit. It takes a compelling cause or motivation to consider change. That's what a passionate concern for people and their eternal welfare does in Gospel movements. It opens the door of possibility for new methods in order to accomplish the central purpose of sharing the Good News of Jesus Christ. But if the new methods overshadow or erode the central truth, the imbalance will hinder the movement of the Gospel. And if the "stubborn

---

[88] Addison, *Movements*, 114.

intransigence"—the resistance to any change—prevents the development of new methods, the Gospel light will be put under a bushel, rarely to be seen by anyone. Adaptability means balance.

Steve Addison captured this delicate but necessary balance when he said, "Adaptive methods are recognized by their fruit. These methods are functional, responsive, simple, sustainable and resilient. Adaptive methods enable a movement to function in ways that suit its changing environment and its expansion into new fields. Movements that drift away from their core beliefs are always at risk, but so are movements that regard the way they currently function as sacred."[89]

Adaptability is a both/and proposition: Both being tenacious about the truth and being daring about outreach coexist; both tradition and innovation walk together; both the old and the new inhabit the life of the movement. This requires a great deal of trust, communication, accountability and intentionality. People from different generations need to love each other. Individuals with differing opinions and preferences need to give each other the benefit of the doubt. Common values and beliefs need to be reinforced over and over again while permission is given to stretch into new areas by doing new things. If a church does not steward this balance carefully, decline can set in. Addison wisely noted:

> When powerful organizations and movements in one era end up crippled in the next, the cause is often "the failure of success." They become so convinced what they are doing is right that they stop paying attention to the world around them. They stop learning and adapting. Worse still, the informal methods that brought the initial success become formalized in inflexible and complex policies and procedures. Creativity and innovation jump ship or are made to walk the plank. There is a cure for movements that have lost touch with a changing world. They must revisit their core beliefs and then give the young and the young at heart freedom to pioneer something new.[90]

---

[89] Addison, *Movements*, 108.
[90] Addison, *Movements*, 110.

God's Adaptability

This is what God has always done. He doesn't change, but He does adapt. When Adam and Eve disobeyed Him by eating of the fruit of the tree of the knowledge of good and evil, God adapted in order to complete His loving plan for His precious people. When Abraham pleaded for Sodom and Gomorrah, God adapted. He told Abraham that He would spare the cities for the sake of ten believers. When Moses decided to take deliverance into his hands as he killed an Egyptian and, consequently, alienated everyone around him, God adapted. He waited an additional thirty years to work His plan of deliverance through a humbled and rehabilitated Moses. When the people of Israel persistently disobeyed God's call to be a light for the nations by mistreating the poor and lowly, God adapted. He sent His prophets to call the people back to the core of His will. He said through the prophet Micah: "With what shall I come before the Lord, and bow myself before God on high? ...He has told you, O man, what is good; and what does the Lord require of you but to do justice, and to love kindness, and to walk humbly with your God?" (Micah 6:6, 8)

The sending of His Only Son was an act of God's adaptation rooted in Genesis chapter three. Jesus reflected the heart of God as He never changed His Father's plan, but adapted to people in need. He witnessed to the woman at the well (John 4). He healed the daughter of the Canaanite woman who begged for a miracle (Matthew 15). He healed on the Sabbath, ate with tax collectors and sinners, fed thousands when they stayed too late listening to Him, and even appeared to the Apostle John in order to redirect the churches in Asia Minor when they went off the rails. Jesus adapted.

Why would we do anything less? Peter realized he needed to enter into fellowship with the Gentiles. The Jerusalem Council realized they shouldn't make it difficult for Gentiles to become part of the church. How do you need to adapt? How do you need to carefully balance solid truth with new methods that will reach your generation with the Gospel? This requires wisdom, humility and

151

sacrifice. Steve Addison gives us marching orders, a challenge to facilitate a movement of the Gospel:

> To fulfill their mission, the most effective movements are prepared to change everything about themselves except their basic beliefs. Unencumbered by tradition, movements feel free to experiment with new forms of the church and new effective methods of ministry. Movements embody their vision and values in systems that are effective, flexible and reproducible, outlasting and even surpassing the influence of the first generation of leaders.[91]

How are we being called to adapt in order to catalyze a Gospel movement in the United States? What areas of ministry might we need to adjust in order to show Jesus' love and care to all people by bringing them the beautiful, freeing, and hope-giving truth of the Gospel? By the grace of God and the power of the Holy Spirit, some pioneers are showing us the way.

---

[91] Addison, *Movements*, 116-117.

Questions for Discussion – Chapter Sixteen

1. What impresses you about and makes you thankful for God's adaptability?

2. Discuss the balance between tradition and innovation needed for healthy adaptability. What makes you most nervous about this? What excites you the most?

3. Steve Addison commented about how organizations can move forward: "They must revisit their core beliefs and then give the young and the young at heart freedom to pioneer something new." What are some ways you can give the young and young at heart freedom to pioneer something new for the cause of the Gospel?

4. What implications might Steve Addison's quote on page 152 have for the church or for your local congregation today?

5. Discuss the two closing questions of this chapter on page 152.

Gospel DNA Journal:

How I've seen God's unique reach into my life…

What changes God has worked and is working in me…

Chapter Seventeen
Adaptability in Action Today

*"It is my judgment, therefore, that we should not make it difficult
for the Gentiles who are turning to God."*
The Apostle James speaking at the Jerusalem Council in Acts
15:19 (NIV)

Pioneers in Adaptability

The United States is blessed with hundreds of thousands of Christian Churches. Some are small faith communities where most everyone knows each other. Others are mega-churches with full staffs and a complete complement of programs and ministries. These churches are bringing the love of Jesus to millions of people locally and around the world. They are serving in their communities, sending people on mission trips, walking with the elderly and young people, encouraging moms, keeping men accountable, teaching children, and bearing witness to the presence of God through their words and actions.

But, for a significant percentage of people in the United States, the church experience is not on the radar. Some are not interested in participating. Others are suspicious about the church as an institution. If people are looking to participate in church at all, they are looking for expressions of the Christian life that reflect what they live and know every day. They are seeking dialog, service that makes a difference, contexts that are more natural for their circles of relationships, and communication methods that reflect their varied media styles. They're also seeking what the world can't give: transcendence. They need a sense of wonder. They are seeking, perhaps, a twenty-first century version of the church in the book of Acts where the new followers of Jesus lived life together in a supernatural and supportive way. Acts chapter 2 tells us:

And they devoted themselves to the apostles' teaching and the fellowship, to the breaking of bread and the prayers. And awe came upon every soul, and many wonders and signs were being done through the apostles. And all who believed were together and had all things in common. And they were selling their possessions and belongings and distributing the proceeds to all, as any had need. And day by day, attending the temple together and breaking bread in their homes, they received their food with glad and generous hearts, praising God and having favor with all the people. And the Lord added to their number day by day those who were being saved (Acts 2:42–47).

Can the church adapt its methods to reach new people? Led by the Holy Spirit, it's happening around our nation. I see "embryonic" churches being developed by new generations of believers in new places. Formerly homeless young people are starting faith walks and beginning to serve youth in the position they once were in. They're starting to enter into communities called "families" because they've never had families before. They are embodying key characteristics of what it means to be the church. How did this happen? A caring couple met them where they were at, loved them, helped them with real needs, and connected what they were doing to God's amazing work of grace. These once broken and hopeless twenty-somethings were far from what a conventional church might be able to handle. The life-gap was too large. Access seemed impossible. But now a new entry point for being part of the family of God has opened up. They're experiencing church in ways they understand, in a context that's familiar, and in a manner that engages them as respected and redeemed people of God.

In a small town, a recovering addict has started a weekly gathering and is hanging out near gambling halls in order to talk to patrons about the Way and the Truth and the Life. She was embraced, baptized, discipled and sent by a missionary couple in their twenties who started a multi-location ministry in a county being impacted by the oil boom. This new missionary never had a voice in her community and was never allowed a voice in a church. Now she is reaching people to whom the conventional church has absolutely no access.

An urban ministry has turned a homeless shelter into "church" for residents as they enjoy fellowship, spiritual retreats, eating together, prayer and worship. The residents and clients would likely have been seen only as "projects" or nuisances by traditional churches, so the church came to them in a way that was embracing, joyful, respectful and natural. One former resident is now living in an apartment and has a job. He was baptized and asked the ministry leaders to join them in serving at the shelter. They welcomed him as a fellow servant to reach precious people with the Gospel.

Middle Eastern immigrant women are meeting with their peers in several urban apartment complexes to welcome newcomers, eat together, converse, and learn how to sew. They are living out the love of Jesus—and talking about Him, too. There is no church building or formal script, but they are becoming the church. Men are not allowed to give instruction to Muslim women, so women are leading the way in gently sharing the hope and beauty of life in Jesus Christ. More than 25,000 refugees are packed into one-hundred apartment complexes in this dense urban area. Because of language and transportation barriers, most of these immigrants would have no access to a typical church. Once again, the gap is wide, so the people would remain unreached. But this urban ministry wants to become a presence in every apartment complex in the area so all people can have a chance to experience the power of Jesus' resurrection and the miracle of His love.

In another large metropolitan area, immigrants who have had theological training abroad are being connected to a local mission network for training and deployment. They begin by reaching their own people groups and expand the mission by reaching neighborhoods, schools and workplaces. Communities are being renewed. Residents are being served. New people are being formed and sent locally to impact local needs and relationships. Gatherings are happening in homes, apartment courtyards, and old unused churches. More than thirty churches have been planted. Fifteen different languages are used in the spectrum of these gatherings. New multiplying leaders are being raised up and sent. The seeds of a Gospel movement are beginning to germinate. Through the love and presence of Jesus, lives are being changed.

As headlines decry the religiosity of millennials, a resurgence of faith in Jesus is happening in a hip metro area among twenty-somethings. It all started when two coffee baristas who worked on Sundays asked a local missionary if he could bring church to them in the coffee shop. He said yes. Now, young lives are being changed. A girl who led a difficult life and felt unwanted got connected with the coffee shop group. Jesus picked her up in her brokenness and she is now a brand new person. Dozens of the "lost generation" gather, invite, include and embrace fellow millennials. This "accidental church" is now beginning to replicate across the city with three young people in their twenties at the helm. The Holy Spirit opened the door; missionaries were willing to adapt; new people are being rescued, repaired and released to bring the church to people they care about.

I can go on and on about the remarkable movement of the Gospel: regular people reaching others in poor neighborhoods, neighbors bringing Christ-teaching children's activities from house to house, adults training and sending middle-schoolers to witness to and mentor their peers, a caring woman sharing ice-cream with kids in an apartment complex instead of waiting for families to come to church, church members giving driving lessons to new immigrants, small churches befriending public school staffs, an inner city ministry teaching public school children leadership and forming relationships with them and their families, a local missionary becoming a volunteer fire-fighter and shining Christ's light in the department, an evangelist connecting with people at town festivals in rural America, and nurses and doctors bringing needed medical help to the forgotten and marginalized. Pioneers are adapting methods to bring the transformational and eternal hope-giving love and power of God to all. Much more is possible. Bridges can replace barriers when people adapt eternal truths to new contexts.

Go!

When Jesus said, "Go!", adapting to new contexts became part of the marching orders. The Apostle Paul said, "I have become all things to all people, that by all means I might save some" (1 Corinthians 9:22). You remember what Rosaria Butterfield said about what Pastor Ken Smith did for her: "Ken, of course, knows the power of the word preached but it seemed to me he also knew at that time that I couldn't come to church— it would have been too threatening, too weird, too much. So, Ken was willing to bring the church to me."[92] He brought the church to her. He heeded Jesus' command to "Go!". Rosaria Butterfield was very clear about the fact that Pastor Ken Smith did not capitulate. He did not try to massage God's Word so it said what everyone wanted to hear. No, he was a person of the truth. He knew the truth brought miraculous freedom and abounding grace. But he did adapt the way he brought the truth. In relationship, for the sake of the Gospel, because he cared deeply about this activist professor, he adapted. He was a pioneer for a new context in a new generation. How might we follow in the courageous and wise steps of these pioneers? It may start by considering seven factors that are crying out for change in our generation.

---

[92] Butterfield, *Secret Thoughts*, Kindle Location 316-320.

Questions for Discussion – Chapter Seventeen

1. What new thoughts about adaptability did this chapter give you?

2. How should and shouldn't the shifting cultural perception of the church lead the church to make changes?

3. What mission and ministry stories in this chapter resonated with you? Why? What ideas do they give you about reaching people for Jesus in your context?

4. Ken Smith's outreach is described in this way: "In relationship, for the sake of the Gospel, because he cared deeply about this activist professor, he adapted. He was a pioneer for a new context in a new generation." How is God leading you and your church to do the same?

5. What "embryonic" churches have the potential of being started in your context? How might these new ministries work with existing churches to foster expanded Gospel outreach?

Gospel DNA Journal:

How God has made me a pioneer in my context and with my gifts...

I am grateful for these Gospel pioneers...

Chapter Eighteen
Where the Spirit is Leading Change

"Behold, I am doing a new thing; now it springs forth, do you not perceive it? I will make a way in the wilderness and rivers in the desert."
God's Word to the people in Isaiah 43:19

Change

    "Change." The word may strike fear in your heart. You may not want to change. You may be completely uncomfortable with change. But you may need to do it. Why are 56% of people sixty-five years of age and older on Facebook—a social media phenomenon limited to college students just over a decade ago?[93] Because access to information has changed. Grandmas and grandpas need to connect if they want to see the latest news about their loved ones' lives. Writing letters is a very nice practice, but it won't bring the immediate connection a social media video will bring. Phone calls are great, but a high percentage of Gen-Xers and millennials won't answer their phones. They prefer text messages or contact through social media. The result? Many older adults have changed. They've adapted. Their core value of loving family remains strong, but their methods needed to change.

    What needs to change in the church? How are we, the family of faith in our Lord Jesus Christ, being called to adapt these days? What are some key adaptations that may help the truth to be told, our stories of life-transformation to be shared, and the movement of the Gospel to take hold in a culture that isn't very interested in the Christian Church? Let's look at seven areas.

---

[93] Felix Richter, "Social Seniors Flock to Facebook," https://www.statista.com/chart/3120/social-media-adoption-by-us-adults/.

The Expression of Church

As you saw in the previous chapter, new expressions of church are being brought to people who wouldn't visit existing churches. Elements of the fullness of Christ's Church from the New Testament are being delivered and implemented among groups of overlooked people. Instead of waiting for people to walk through the doorways of church buildings, and instead of becoming paralyzed by a culture that confuses us, pioneers are faithfully carrying what it means to be the church into the plentiful harvest. New expressions of church open new pathways for the saving Gospel to enter unreached lives.

David Garrison noted how house gatherings in a global south community opened doors for a Gospel movement no one could have imagined. He said: "Moving the churches into homes as casas cultos, or house churches, stimulated several things simultaneously. It freed the church from identification with buildings. It necessitated far more leaders than the seminaries could provide—provoking a major lay leadership movement. It eliminated any time delay in starting a new church. Many from Roman Catholic or atheist backgrounds felt uncomfortable entering a...church building, but were less threatened by visiting a neighbor's home. It allowed the movement to grow rapidly without attracting immediate public notice or government censure that would certainly have come if new church buildings had been constructed."[94]

New expressions of church increase the bandwidth of access to the Gospel. I am not talking about groups that try to escape the church or rebel against the church. I am talking about the fullness of biblical church occupying locations and happening among groups of people in a variety of sizes, locations, and structures. The Holy Spirit is leading us into this type of adaptation during this generation. What new expressions of church do you see the Holy Spirit prompting?

---

[94] Garrison, *Church Planting Movements*, Kindle Locations 1985-1991.

The Church's Presence in the Community

Some people gladly come to church. Where I live, about twenty-percent of the population is inclined to attend church on a weekend. That means that eighty-percent of the population has little regular contact with the church. If the gift of eternal life in Jesus Christ is important for everyone, how will more people come into contact with the living and breathing body of Christ? Can the church limit its presence to its building and programs? The answer has always been, "No."

Internal forces are always at work, pushing the church behind closed doors. The question that needs to be asked over and over again by the church is: How can we be present effectively and winsomely in the community?

Some may say, "But we try to reach the community and our attendance doesn't grow." The point of being present in the community is not to boost attendance. It is to demonstrate and share the love of Jesus. It is the church in action, boldly claiming the entire community as its responsibility. Every person, business, non-profit, school and neighborhood group is under the lordship of Jesus Christ. The church embraces everything—just as "The earth is the Lord's and the fullness thereof, the world and those who dwell therein" (Psalms 24:1). Everything is the church's—even if everyone doesn't know it yet. The metric of attendance in a church building may or may not grow, but the metric of claiming the community for Christ and reaching into every corner of your region will bring the Gospel far and wide. And the power of the Gospel will make a difference.

The church cannot retreat from the community or be a bystander while the community does its thing. The church IN the world must be IN the community deeply and meaningfully.

Educational Systems

Jesus requested prayer for more workers in the harvest field. He said, "The harvest is plentiful, but the laborers are few. Therefore pray earnestly to the Lord of the harvest to send out laborers into his harvest" (Luke 10:2). Jesus expressed the need for people to carry into His storehouses what He is growing by His grace through the Holy Spirit. The crop is ready in abundance. The only thing lacking is workers.

In order to prepare church workers, my denomination has adopted a rigorous educational process rooted in European university and graduate education. Training and formation take place at accredited institutions. Students earn degrees and are placed in ministries by placement committees. The system has some wonderful strengths and has served the church for decades. But it has never been able to keep up with an expanding church—with a movement. It is complex, expensive and rigorous. Adaptation is critical for reaching the plentiful harvest rapidly with locally developed workers who learn in the contexts of their relationships and communities. The current system should not be eliminated, but it needs to be supplemented for the sake of a Gospel movement. Fortunately, some simplification and streamlining through distance learning programs has taken place. But beyond an ordained clergy level of worker, multiple levels of Gospel workers need to be developed that allow formation and deployment to happen in a faster, less costly, more inclusive, and more locally focused way. Some of these workers will never take steps toward ordination. A number, however, will develop competencies and an appetite for additional education. Expanded educational systems will not threaten ordained ministry. They will increase the need for able and well prepared pastors, they will expand the supply of high quality candidates, and they will add the many workers needed to reach the plentiful harvest.

Communication Methods

Communication methods are always changing. People are accessing information in new ways and communicating with one another through a variety of platforms. How does the church need to adapt? How can the church use new communication methods to reach a new generation and to maximize Gospel outreach? For some, customary worship services and communication methods are most comfortable. For others, new communication methods are essential—not only as a preference but because they cannot understand communication methods of the past. Attention spans are shorter. They need interaction. They crave participation and putting the Word of God into action as part of their worship. They want to ask questions—right now! They want their opinions to be taken seriously. They want dialog. They want real fellowship. They like venues that allow for food and drink, conversation and care. They need shorter bursts of information with time for reflection. They want to be able to access faith resources wherever they are, whatever time it may be.

New communication methods and habits present the church with the possibility of outreach that is exponential. We shouldn't throw away what the church has been doing, but we do need to harness new communication developments so that the changeless Christ can be brought boldly to a changing world.

Ethnic Diversity

In 1963 during a question and answer session after a speech at Western Michigan University, Dr. Martin Luther King, Jr. said, "We must face the fact that in America the church is still the most segregated major institution in America. At 11:00 on Sunday morning when we stand and sing [that] Christ has no east or west, we stand at the most segregated hour in this nation. This is tragic."[95] More than half a century later, research shows that American churchgoers believe their churches are not in need of more ethnic diversity. Dr. Ed Stetzer, Executive Director of LifeWay Research commented: "Surprisingly, most churchgoers are content with the ethnic status quo in their churches. In a world where our culture is increasingly diverse, and many pastors are talking about diversity, it appears most people are happy where they are—and with whom they are."[96]

---

[95] "MLK at Western,"
http://wmich.edu/sites/default/files/attachments/MLK.pdf, p. 22.
[96] Bob Smietana, "Sunday Morning in America Still Segregated – and That's OK With Worshipers," http://lifewayresearch.com/2015/01/15/sunday-

A friend shared with me a quote from one of the leaders in the LCMS in the 1960's. In the very same year Dr. Martin Luther King, Jr. spoke his words at Western Michigan University, Dr. Martin Franzmann said in his book, *New Courage for Daily Living*: "We cannot read these lines without thinking of our snug little parishes in 'nice' sections of the city; they make no rules to keep anybody out, to be sure. But how is it that the not-so-nice people from not-so-nice sections never get in? How is it that these nice parishes remain so uniformly nice year after year – or relocate when the niceness of the neighborhood begins to wear thin?"[97]

Dr. King, Dr. Franzmann, and Dr. Stetzer highlight a pervasive and sinful issue in the Christian Church: racism, discrimination, hatred, unkind words, a paternalistic spirit toward ethnic groups, passive neglect of God's precious people, and active resistance to being churches for every nation, family, people, and tongue (Revelation 7:9).

How we need to repent! This is a blind spot we must recognize and change. We need to surrender our fear and pride, and, in an increasingly ethnic nation, sit at the feet and learn from brothers and sisters of the nations in our midst. We need to give away power and control. We need to be led into multi-ethnic and multi-cultural ministry by leaders who have full authority to exercise adaptability as they communicate the unchanging truth of the Gospel to a changing world.

When Peter said, "I now realize how true it is that God does not show favoritism but accepts men from every nation who fear him and do what is right" (Acts 10:34–35 NIV), he helped open the door not only for the acceptance of the nations, but to give authority to the nations. In Acts chapter 11, the ministry among the Gentiles in Antioch caused a rebranding of the movement of Christ-followers. Previously labeled as "the way," the once-pagan Greeks were now called "Christians." It was a Gentile expression

---

morning-in-america-still-segregated-and-thats-ok-with-worshipers/, January 15, 2015.

[97] Martin Franzmann, *New Courage for Daily Living* (St. Louis: Concordia Publishing House, 1963), 60.

that stuck. Gentile thought was now co-leading the movement of the Gospel through the world.

Fortunately, the Holy Spirit is stirring up in the hearts of the new generation a craving for diversity and inclusion. He is also bringing the world to the United States. In my experience with local missionaries, it is evident that receptivity to the Gospel is much higher among ethnic students and immigrants than among the domestic population. In the church planting efforts of the ministry I serve, more than half of the new churches launched over the past decade use a language other than English. We need to be faithful, self-sacrificial, kind and humble stewards of this Spirit-led development toward diversity.

Funding Models

The cost of ministry is skyrocketing. In addition to the price of real estate, the expense of new construction, and the financial demands of deferred maintenance on existing structures, the church has taken on a corporately modeled staffing system that is pricing local faith communities out of the market. Benefits packages alone are grounding the efforts of churches to call workers. All of this is happening in "middle class" congregations. Developing sustainable models of ministry by under-resourced faith communities has been neglected and ignored. Church is just not affordable for some people. It is a mid to upper class luxury. The poor either have to forego a faith community or live as a "project" of a wealthier patron—abiding by the customs and preferences of that patron.

Funds in the church are diminishing, as well. As the church loses its vision and slips into survival mode, donors seek causes that are on the upswing, that show results, and that focus on mission, not maintenance.

Several changes mentioned previously in educational systems, expressions of church, and ethnic diversity will help create funding models that work. But additional options need to be explored. It is becoming more common to see servants in ministry who work in both the marketplace and in the church. Returnable seed money for starting new churches is a funding model being used by a number of networks around the nation—including the ministry in which I serve. God will provide for His church, but we must be wise and faithful stewards as we follow where the Spirit leads.

Lanes for Ministry

Dr. Ed Stetzer emphasized to constituents of the LCMS, "If you want to plant more churches, you need more lanes for ministry." He compared the situation to a grocery store. Fewer open checkout lanes meant fewer customers served. More lanes meant the flow of customers could be plentiful. We need more lanes for ministry so more workers can reap the harvest God is growing.

The history of my denomination shows willingness to develop and deploy new ministry positions. You'll see the details in the next chapter. If a movement of the Gospel is to take hold, we need to learn from previous movements in our own nation and current movements around the world. In the Ethiopian Evangelical Church Mekane Yesus, General Secretary, Dr. Berhanu Ofgaa noted several categories of trained and deployed ministry workers. In addition to ordained pastors and full-time evangelists, the church identifies, disciples and sends lay-evangelists, lay-ministers, volunteers (a specific category), extraordinarily gifted people (people who demonstrate special gifts of the Holy Spirit), and committed members. The results are astounding. The church has nearly 10,000 congregations and preaching places, but only about 3,500 pastors. More than than 6,000 full-time evangelists combine efforts with nearly 550,000 volunteers to share the Gospel and disciple new believers. The 7.8-million-member church body wants to share the Gospel with 30 million people, win 10 million converts, and plant 8,000 congregations and 5,000 mission posts in the next five years. They also want to train 1 million new lay leaders.[98]

---

[98] Ofgaa, "The Lay Mission Movement in the Ethiopian Evangelical Church Mekane Yesus."

The Holy Spirit is showing us that opening ministry lanes can lead to a movement of the Gospel. Will we follow? We did at one time, and we experienced remarkable results.

Questions for Discussion – Chapter Eighteen

1. What thoughts did this chapter stir in you?

2. Discuss how adaptation in the seven areas mentioned in this chapter might apply to your context:

    a. The Expression of Church

    b. The Church's Presence in the Community

    c. Educational Systems

    d. Communication Methods

    e. Ethnic Diversity

    f. Funding Models

    g. Lanes for Ministry

3. Read Isaiah 43:19. How does the message of new life from our Savior motivate adaptation and change?

4. Discuss how the truth of the Gospel can be preserved and promoted even as adaptation takes place in the areas mentioned above.

Gospel DNA Journal:

How I think the church needs to change…

What unchanging qualities I appreciate in the church…

Chapter Nineteen

Adaptability During a Gospel Movement

"Look to the rock from which you were hewn, and to the quarry from which you were dug."
Isaiah 51:1

Change That Triggered a Movement

As mentioned in the previous chapter, examples of adaptability in the Missouri Synod abound. The balance of changelessness and change was struck well during the movements of the 1800s and 1900s. From our twenty-first century vantage point, we may not view what these early leaders did as revolutionary. But the courage and sacrifice it took to adapt to a new context, a new nation, and new cultural and technological developments cannot be underestimated. The results of their visionary and faithful actions stand as proof for adaptability as a key marker of Gospel DNA. Let's look at how they followed the Holy Spirit's lead to reach far and wide with the Gospel during their time and in their context. What follows is just a sampling of the overwhelming evidence of how the LCMS became all things to all people so that some might be saved.

The Expression of Church

Rev. A.W. Kraft graduated from Concordia Theological Seminary, Springfield, Illinois in June of 1900. Because he wasn't yet twenty-one years old, he had to find other work before he could be called to serve a congregation. After waiting, he was called to serve in South Dakota and was ordained and installed in July of that year. Kraft lived in a granary and led services in a local home. He was also given permission to start area preaching stations and to develop ministry among local Native Americans. Kraft received his education in the German language but knew that English was the language of the future for new generations. He navigated the tumultuous transition to English along with learning Spanish for additional ethnic outreach.[99] This was the norm for a pastor on the frontier. He adapted to conditions and contexts—so often with complete self-sacrifice—in order to bring the church to people who needed the Gospel.

The expression of church was varied and flexible. Ministry efforts were made in prisons, urban areas, and hospitals. Preaching stations were begun through relationships and outreach. Numbers may have been small, but the goal was to plant seeds of the Gospel. Homes and public buildings were gathering points. Relationships around dialog, food, fellowship, prayer, study, serving others and worshiping together formed the structure of a preaching station. Sometimes the pastor and faithful laypeople would travel together for days to bring the Gospel far and wide into new contexts and communities. They took personal time to bring the church where it was needed.

Then, media began to take the nation by storm. The radio was born. In 1924, Walter A. Maier considered the possibility of using the radio for ministry. Many were against utilizing this new technology to proclaim the Gospel. But Maier's thoughts reflected Gospel movement thinking, the DNA of adaptability for the sake of the Good News of Jesus Christ. He said, "And what about those who can't attend church because of illness, or age, or location? Now the church can come to them wherever they may be."[100] The church can come to them. The Holy Spirit opened the door for the increased bandwidth of the Gospel to world.

The Church's Presence in the Community

In the late 1930s, the depression severely restricted the ability of churches to afford pastors. In 1937, only one new graduate received an assignment to a church. Candidate C. D. Uetzmann didn't receive that ministry call, so he went to work

---

[99] Gertrude Ring, "My Dad—Lutheran Minister 1900-1950" (Paper shared by Rev. Tim Radkey, McKinney, Texas, 2016).
[100] Maier, *A Man Spoke*, p. 70.

selling books for Concordia Publishing House, the LCMS publishing arm. After several months, the synod asked Uetzmann to serve at a community church in a small North Dakota town. This was not a Lutheran Church. Pastor Uetzmann's job was to serve as pastor, get to know the people, and become involved in the community. Perhaps he could reach people with the Gospel and the church would become part of the LCMS. Uetzmann got to work. He played his trumpet in the town band. He became the town's justice of the peace. As his faithful and diligent service went on, the people of the church and of the community were won over. In time, the community church joined the Lutheran Church–Missouri Synod. Pastor Uetzmann's marching orders were to adapt, to approach his church and community with a spirit of Gospel-focused flexibility. In time, his presence in the community was a decisive factor for the movement of the Gospel there.

During the years when German immigrants were pouring into the United States, the Missouri Synod brought a strong ministry presence to the ports. Missionaries were stationed at the boat docks. They were there to greet the German people in their own language and to offer a helping hand. Many new immigrants who had no church connection and no intention of becoming part of a church were referred to welcoming followers of Christ in LCMS churches around the country. These new friends provided places to stay, food to eat, and resources to find jobs. They also shared the Good News of Jesus Christ.

Even the people who were determined to keep to themselves were swept up in adapting to a new nation. In 1854, Rev. Jan Killian arrived in Galveston with a band of Wendish immigrants. They wanted to live in a new land where they could preserve their language and culture. But they realized quickly that they couldn't function alone. After seeing C.F.W. Walther's publication, "Lehre und Wehre" (Teaching and Defending), Killian applied for membership in the Missouri Synod. As economic and social realities of the new land set in, the Wends found themselves spreading the Gospel not only in the Wendish and German languages, but even in English. The Wends adapted—by the Spirit and grace of God. They also catalyzed a movement of the Gospel as they planted churches throughout Texas.[101]

Educational Systems

The Missouri Synod imported its pastoral formation system from Europe. It took nine years to educate and develop a pastor in the early days of the church's presence in the United States. It became evident very soon that the need was far greater than the supply, so hundreds of pastors were sent to the U.S. from Germany to help serve the growing population and the rapidly expanding church.

Rev. Wilhelm Loehe, who trained missionaries around his kitchen table and sent them to the United States as "emergency helpers," worked to establish local training for missionaries. He and his men started the "practical seminary" in 1846 in Fort Wayne, Indiana.   The goal of this seminary was to train and deploy missionary pastors as quickly as possible so no souls were lost.   The Gospel DNA marker of adaptability was evident. Historian Carl Meyer noted: "More than half of those who graduated from the seminary in Fort Wayne during the first nine years of the school's existence attended from one to two years; about a third of them, two to three years. The aim was to provide men with the most practical instruction so that they would enter the work as early as possible."[102]

Later in history, the LCMS released men from the seminary early because the need for pastors was so great. Adaptability showed up in the international mission field, as well. W.H.T. Dau mentioned an on-the-mission-field ordination of a local worker in India: "Indeed, a bright day of great rejoicing for the missionaries and their charges was the second Sunday in March, 1921. Jesudason, who under God was instrumental in bringing the missionaries to the field in Travancore, and who for years was educated and trained by them, and tried by practical

---

[101] Ron Lammert, "Who Are The Wends?" (San Antonio: Lammert Publishing).

[102] Meyer, *Moving Frontiers*, 217.

service as an evangelist, after having passed very creditably a thorough examination before the missionary conference, was, pursuant to a resolution of the Board, ordained to the ministry, and as 'Indian pastor' was given his own mission-charge."[103]

Educational systems became a specialty of the LCMS. With the goal of seeing lives transformed by the Gospel, the Missouri Synod set out to establish strong and effective discipleship for its members. Even before the formal creation of a synod, the Lutherans launched schools. From grade school through seminary, young people were to be taught and nurtured in the truth of God's Word. Workers for ministry were shaped and inspired. Christian adults were sent into the world to shine Christ's light through their vocations. By its 100th anniversary, the LCMS claimed over 1000 Christian elementary schools, twelve colleges in North and South America, four colleges for the preparation of teachers, four seminaries in the United States and Canada, and church worker formation institutions in India and China. In many ways, through a variety of methods, people were being discipled and sent as bearers of the truth. This was the DNA of the Missouri Synod.

Communication Methods

A movement-oriented church adapts its communication methods. The Missouri Synod bore evidence of this Spirit-led DNA marker. In his 1919 book, *The Practical Missionary*, Rev. John H.C. Fritz discussed how communication in a worship service needs to be adjusted for new believers gathering during the initial formation stages of a church. He said, "To begin with…a simple order of service should be used: hymn, Scripture lesson, hymn, sermon, hymn, collect, benediction, doxology."[104] Fritz emphasized that the missionary needed to reflect the love of Jesus and extend a gracious personal welcome. He should be sure to include hymns and hymn tunes that were familiar to the people. Fritz understood that the full liturgical tradition in the Lutheran

---

[103] Dau, *Ebenezer*, 398-399.
[104] Fritz, *The Practical Missionary*, 36.

Church could be too much and too difficult for beginners. The focus was on Christ. People could learn traditions in time.

The defining season of communication breakthroughs for the LCMS materialized when the Lutheran Hour radio broadcast was ushered in under the leadership of Dr. Walter A. Maier. When the possibility of preaching over the radio surfaced, a number of people voiced doubt and fear. Would people stop coming to church if they could access sermons on the radio? Maier's thinking set the stage for the second Gospel movement of the LCMS. Instead of doubt and fear, he expressed wonder and embraced possibilities. He said, "Imagine the implications—masses could hear and even be brought to faith."[105]

When television came on the scene, the International Lutheran Laymen's League—the ministry sponsor of the Lutheran Hour—created "This is the Life," a cutting edge television series that blended contemporary challenges with spiritual themes. The show ran from 1952 to 1988. Story lines ventured into themes that perplexed and vexed a nation: addiction, racism, marital infidelity, war and grief.[106] Blogger Caroline Langston recalls an episode of "This is the Life" that changed her forever. She was a teenager when "This is the Life" told the story of an African American family that welcomed a white teenage boy as a foster child. The angry young boy was rude and thoroughly racist. He looked with scorn at his foster family and acted out his rebellious defiance. But when the young daughter of the family was victimized, the boy realized that she, too, was a human being worthy of love and respect. His heart was changed. Langston reflected on the moving story: "It made me want the racial chasm all around me to be healed, but even more (I identified, you see, with that angry white teenaged boy), it convinced me of the reality of sin, my need to be redeemed. And it also convinced me of the reality of mysterious, unexpected grace."[107] The communication methods of the LCMS

---

[105] Maier, *A Man Spoke*, 70.

[106] "This is the Life," http://www.imdb.com/title/tt0136671/.

[107] Sojourners, "This is the Life: The Lost Episode," February 15, 2012, http://sojo.net/blogs/2012/02/15/life-lost-episode.

engaged in bold adaptability in order to see the Gospel move into difficult places and touch unreached lives.

Ethnic Diversity

From its very beginning the Missouri Synod was actively involved in outreach to Native Americans. That was a primary purpose of the missionaries sent by Loehe. In 1852, Loehe pushed for more ethnic outreach. The LCMS agreed with his plan to send workers to "give attention and spiritual care not only to German emigrants in California but also to the great number of Chinese who were immigrating there."[108] By 1860, the synod was able to send an English speaking missionary to California to answer the many pleas for mission support.

While the LCMS was thoroughly German in language and tradition, the church tried its best to connect with people of many cultures who were living in the United States. As awareness of the "melting pot" nation grew, the Missouri Synod sent missionaries to work in urban areas, among Jewish populations, with Middle Eastern people, in the development of ministry among African Americans, and with the Hispanic population. International outreach also grew and developed. Mission fields opened in China, India, and South America. By 1920, the LCMS mission in India numbered 66 mission stations, 4,180 souls, 2,401 baptized members, 68 schools with 3,049 pupils (609 were baptized, 2,440 were not), and 303 received into the church by baptism that year.[109]

The LCMS conscience was also being stirred regarding its work in the English language. During the synod's early development, an emphasis on diversity meant assimilating with the English-speaking culture. Ultimately, the Missouri Synod was forced to make a change as the anti-German sentiment of World War I swept the nation. Long before that time, however, C.F.W. Walther confessed, "God has brought us into this country and without our merit has given us that pure doctrine also for the purpose that we should spread it in the language of our country.

---

[108] Meyer, *Moving Frontiers*, 197.
[109] Dau, *Ebenezer*, 401-402.

But, alas! we did not do what we should have done, and I fear God will punish us for our negligence and take away from us Germans the great blessings which He bestowed upon us because we did not do in the English Language what we should have done."[110]   Why was the English language so important to the church?   LCMS Vice-President Brohm commented in 1872, "Moreover, as Synod becomes stronger, it must make more generous provisions for the English language…that our members may be better equipped in a larger sphere to fulfil their heavenly calling of being a light in the Lord and that they thus also as Christian citizens may help to promote the welfare of our country."[111]   The German language was important for work with first-generation immigrants and for accurate communication of the truths of the faith.   But times were changing.

Following World War I, the outcry for English intensified. Carl Giesler, quoting Professor Theodore Graebner, emphasized that the movement of the Gospel depended on it: "The religious instruction of our children should, as a rule, be in English and not in German (at least not exclusively), otherwise the religious knowledge of the coming generation will be locked up in a safe to which it has lost the combination."[112]

Funding Models

A movement of the Gospel adapts.   Sometimes the adaptation takes place because of desperation.   In 1917, the LCMS needed $100,000 to settle a debt.   The church was strapped.   No resources were to be found.   That's when a group of twelve men decided to impact the funding model of the LCMS in a generous and entrepreneurial way.   While meeting in Milwaukee at a convention of the church body, the men formed the Lutheran Laymen's League.   They personally contributed the funds and bailed out their beloved church body.   That, however, was just the beginning.   Word spread and more men were recruited to make a

---

[110] Meyer, *Torch Bearers*, 12.

[111] Meyer, *Torch Bearers*., 12.

[112] Giesler, *The Wide-Open Island City*, 35.

financial difference in the church. Their next step was to raise more than $2.7 million to fund a pension plan for pastors and teachers.[113] That would equal raising nearly $34 million today. A lay movement for independently and directly funding ministry was born. Out of that lay movement grew the media ministry that transformed the LCMS into an American evangelistic movement of the Gospel. The new funding model opened remarkable doors.

The Synod's collaborative partnership as congregations to gather offerings for mission work caused a significant expansion of the work of the church. Local congregations contributed funds to launch missions locally and internationally. Churches pooled resources in order to fund colleges and seminaries. Suddenly the synod was able to think bigger and more broadly. The synod discovered the power of working together. This new funding model catapulted the Gospel's reach to the ends of the earth.

Lanes for Ministry

From early on, mission-focused LCMS leaders appealed for the expansion of ministry lanes. In an 1856 request to the LCMS convention, Rev. Carl Selle of the Western District wrote of the current sacrifice of pastors in an expanding nation and the need for additional workers: "This call [the call of love] also many pastors of our Synod have followed and before and since its founding have carried the joyous message often and far beyond the boundaries of their congregations...Therefore no one should allow himself to be restrained by false conscientiousness, as if his call went no further than only the specific congregation which has called him as its pastor. No matter how much can and should be done in this way, our vision must extend farther...Now, we believe that we can do this by establishing the so-called office of evangelist; those who hold this office should not bind themselves to this or that congregation or congregations, but they shall make it

---

[113] "Our History," Lutheran Hour Ministries, Accessed March 30, 2016, http://www.lhm.org/about/ourhistory.asp.

their only task to plant the church...where it does not yet exist..."[114]

In addition to the desire for evangelists, the LCMS already sanctioned several ministry lanes for the ever-growing mission efforts. "Book Agents" (called colporteurs) were sent to scour communities by going door-to-door, offering Christian books to families and asking about a connection with a church. "Traveling Preachers" (Reiseprediger) combed communities to discover entry points for the Gospel. They gathered people for worship and teaching, and they equipped families to conduct ministry in homes and public places. "Visitors" also went from community to community looking for believers and trying to initiate the beginnings of churches.

C.F.W. Walther wrote that all offices entrusted to people for special ministry in the church are "to be regarded as ecclesiastical and sacred, for they take over a part of the one ministry of the Word." He mentioned a variety of ministry "lanes": deacons, teachers, almoners (those who help the poor), sextons (a facility superintendent), and leaders of singing at public worship.[115] The early LCMS didn't consider a variety of ministry lanes threatening to the pastoral office. On the contrary, the church supported multiple offices for the movement of the Gospel.

In the early 1920s, wives of missionaries were labeled as "Associate Missionaries." The service of women was lifted up as many women made greater inroads than men in international mission fields. Nurse Lula Ellerman was lauded as a key mission leader in India who fostered Gospel relationships with thousands of local people.[116] Lanes for ministry in the international mission field were plentiful. A 1921 mission report mentions missionaries, native aids, evangelists, catechists, and teachers.[117] As local mission work increased in the U.S., the position of Field Secretary

---

[114] Meyer, *Moving Frontiers*, 204-205.

[115] *Walther on the Church*, John M. Drickamer, trans. (St. Louis: Concordia Publishing House, 1981), 103-104.

[116] Dau, *Ebenezer*, 399.

[117] Dau, *Ebenezer*, 402.

was added as another ministry lane. The Field Secretary was to canvass potential mission outreach areas, be first on the ground to establish a mission presence, publicize mission stories, and solicit support from local churches.[118]

The Rock

In my conversations with retired pastors, one reflected on why his precious church body seemed stalled. He said, "We stopped doing what we do best." Instead of adapting to new ministry opportunities and contexts, the church was stepping back in fear. Instead of releasing the people of the church, their Gospel efforts were being discouraged. While not perfect, and while most certainly flawed, the Missouri Synod was a Gospel movement that knew how to adapt for the sake of the Gospel.

How can we reconnect with this DNA today? Isaiah 51:1 says it well, "Listen to me, you who pursue righteousness, you who seek the Lord: look to the rock from which you were hewn, and to the quarry from which you were dug." What if we begin, once again, to take a hard look at the rock from which we were hewn? What if we learn from the spirit of our past? What if we reconnect with Gospel DNA that propelled a tiny German church into a series of Gospel movements? John H.C. Fritz offered encouraging words in 1919 as he sized up the challenges of changing times: "In short, mission work in the American city today is much more difficult than it has ever been...This is, however, not a reason which should discourage the church worker and the missionary, but, on the contrary, it ought to stimulate him to do more energetic work, redeeming the time because the days are evil. The Gospel is just as powerful as it has ever been, and the promises of God that His Word shall not be preached in vain still hold good."[119]

How might we become better stewards of adaptability? Let's look at some practical steps in the next chapter.

---

[118] Dau, *Ebenezer*, 387-388.
[119] Fritz, *The Practical Missionary*, 16.

Questions for Discussion – Chapter Nineteen

1. What particularly made an impression on you in this chapter?

2. What ministry ideas do the stories from the past in this chapter give you?

3. Carl Selle said, "Therefore no one should allow himself to be restrained by false conscientiousness, as if his call went no further than only the specific congregation which has called him as its pastor." During Selle's time, it was normal for local congregations to stretch into the surrounding regions. What regions or groups of people might you be able to reach in your area?

4. Read Romans 15:18-21. Talk about what it would take to initiate a new ministry in the regions or among the groups of people you mentioned.

5. How did adaptability and truth work together in the movement called the Missouri Synod? How can you apply that to your church?

Gospel DNA Journal:

What I learn from the history of the church...

My thoughts about starting new ministry in new ways...

Chapter Twenty
How to Adapt

"Truly I understand that God shows no partiality, but in every nation anyone who fears him and does what is right is acceptable to him."
The Apostle Peter to fellow Jews in Acts 10:34–35

Becoming a Learner

King David said in Psalm 5:3, "O Lord, in the morning you hear my voice; in the morning I prepare a sacrifice for you and watch." David asked God questions, put forth petitions, and waited for answers. He was determined to pay attention so God could teach him His paths (Psalm 25:4).

How can you know when and how to adapt, to change everything but your basic beliefs or to tweak something you're already doing in order to see a movement of the Gospel take hold? How do you know when to be a pioneer with the truth of the Gospel?

I have one answer for you: pay attention. That's right, just pay attention. God will lead the way. It is that simple and that difficult. Sometimes desperation will push you to change and adapt. At other times, The Holy Spirit will drag you out of paralysis or complacency to new ministry initiatives. Pay attention and follow Him. When you are immersed in the Word of God, you become familiar with His will and work. God's Word tunes you in to the movement of His Spirit. Watch and wait. Be attentive to people, to the community, and to the signs of the times. Be in prayer. Listen to wise followers of Christ around you. Pay close attention to what people are saying—people close to you in ministry and people outside of the ministry in the community.

Pay attention.

In his book, *Movements That Change the World*, Steve Addison quoted Eric Hoffer: "In a time of drastic change, it is the learners who inherit the future. The learned find themselves equipped to live in a world that no longer exists."[120]

Will you and I resolve to be learners?

In Acts chapter 10, the Apostle Peter was the learned one. He knew exactly where God was leading. Pentecost Day showed the Spirit's work to reach the Jewish people. Thousands of Jews from around the world repented and were baptized that day, receiving the Holy Spirit and the forgiveness of sins. More were becoming part of the fellowship every day. As time went on and persecution ebbed and flowed, Peter had seen the Holy Spirit come upon Samaritan believers. He saw how God took one of the most vicious persecutors of the church and changed him into a proclaimer of Jesus. A different direction was taking hold. But Peter never anticipated how this would impact his ministry. It unfolded on the roof of Simon the Tanner's home in Joppa. Acts 10 tells it this way:

[Peter] fell into a trance and saw the heavens opened and something like a great sheet descending, being let down by its four corners upon the earth. In it were all kinds of animals and reptiles and birds of the air. And there came a voice to him: "Rise, Peter; kill and eat." But Peter said, "By no means, Lord; for I have never eaten anything that is common or unclean." And the voice came to him again a second time, "What God has made clean, do not call common." This happened three times, and the thing was taken up at once to heaven (Acts 10:10–16).

God was initiating change. It was time to adapt. Peter was summoned to Cornelius' house where he saw a crowd of Gentiles receive the Gospel message and be anointed by the Holy Spirit. Humbly, Peter admitted, "Truly I understand that God shows no partiality, but in every nation anyone who fears him and does what is right is acceptable to him" (Acts 10:34-35).

---

[120] Addison, *Movements*, 101.

By God's grace and through the power of the Holy Spirit, Peter became a learner. The future of the church began to open up to him.

How do you know when to adapt and what to adapt? Pay attention and follow.

Extruded

Francis Schaeffer articulated the art of paying attention in his essay, "No Little People, No Little Places." He said that entry into a new situation, a change, or an opportunity to adapt, happens by being "extruded" by God into those new places. He used the imagery of a huge metal press, jamming soft metal through a die so it takes a certain shape. Why is it important to pay attention to God? Why let Him initiate adaptability? Read Schaeffer's wisdom:

> God must be allowed to choose when a Christian is ready to be extruded into such a place, for only he knows when a person will be able to have some quietness before him in the midst of increased pressure and responsibility. Quietness and peace before God are more important than any influence a position may seem to give, for we must stay in step with God to have the power of the Holy Spirit. If by taking a bigger place our quietness with God is lost, then to that extent our fellowship with him is broken and we are living in the flesh, and the final result will not be as great, no matter how important the larger place may look in the eyes of other men or in our own eyes.

> I am not talking about laziness; let me make that clear. That is something else, something too which God hates. I am not talking about copping out or dropping out. God's people are to be active, not seeking, on account of some false mystical concept, to sit constantly in the shade of a rock. There is no monasticism in Christianity. We will not be lazy in our relationship with God, because when the Holy Spirit burns, a man is consumed. We can expect to become physically tired in

the midst of battle for our King and Lord; we should not expect all of life to be a vacation. We are talking about quietness before God as we are in his place for us. The size of the place is not important but the consecration in that place is.

One of the loveliest incidents in the early church occurred when Barnabas concluded that Paul was the man of the hour and then had to seek him out because Paul had gone back to Tarsus, his own little place. Paul was not up there nominating himself; he was back in Tarsus, even out of communication as far as we can tell. When Paul called himself "the chief of sinners, . . . not meet to be an apostle" (1 Tim 1:15; 1 Cor 15:9), he was not speaking just for outward form's sake. From what he said elsewhere and from his actions we can see that this was Paul's mentality. Paul, the man of leadership for the whole Gentile world, was perfectly willing to be in Tarsus until God said to him, "This is the moment."[121]

Knowing when and how to adapt means being quiet before God, being attentive to His Word, and listening for God to say, "This is the moment."

A woman called recently to tell me about just such a moment. She was heartbroken about the young people and families missing out on church because of weekend sports tournaments. Finally, she tried something. On a Sunday morning at a sports event, she and some families held an impromptu time of Scripture reading, prayer, singing and devotional conversation. She expected a few people to gather with them on the field, but everyone on the team came with their families. The portable worship experiment lasted only seven or eight minutes, but she saw the Gospel reach people who hadn't heard God's Word in a long time. Could this be a way to reach people who were completely disconnected from the Gospel due to sports schedules? She

---

[121] Francis Schaeffer, "No Little People, No Little Places, http://www.sbts.edu/wp-content/uploads/sites/5/2010/02/sbjt_062_schaeffer.pdf, 65-66.

believed this was the moment to try. In our last conversation, she was pursuing the possibility of asking her church to train "family chaplains" who would lead simple and interactive devotional times at weekend sporting events across the state. These spiritual leaders would be trained, given resources, encouraged, and sent. Stories of God's blessing would be shared with the congregation. Could this work? Could the church be brought to sports families in their contexts? As we talked, she wept over the souls of the young people who were being separated from the blessing of life in Jesus because of weekend sports schedules. She cared. She wanted to multiply ministry. She yearned for the Gospel to move into the lives of those who were spiritually at risk. How could this urgent need be ignored? She was being led to adapt.

Pay attention. Allow room for God's leading and instruction. Humbly be ready to sacrifice everything except the core of the Gospel, the truth about Jesus the Savior, in order to see the Gospel move to new people and into new places.

When Jesus told the parable of the persistent widow in Luke chapter 8, He made it clear that God is doing his job. He is faithful. The big question was for us: "When the Son of Man comes, will he find faith on earth?" (Luke 18:8)

Will we seek Him? Will we pay attention? Will we be taught by Him? Will we care?

That is how this book began and that is how it needs to end. Will we care about what God's heart longs for?

Questions for Discussion – Chapter Twenty

1. What stood out to you in this chapter?

2. You read an Eric Hoffer quote in this chapter: "In a time of drastic change, it is the learners who inherit the future. The learned find themselves equipped to live in a world that no longer exists." What does this mean and who might you need to learn from these days?

3. What is happening in your life and context that is leading you to be a learner?

4. Read Matthew 6:31-34. What call to action and what promise from Jesus do these verses give you? How might they apply to the way you pay attention to God's guidance and leadership?

5. What confidence, comfort and hope do you have as you venture into the risk of adaptability?

Gospel DNA Journal:

Learning opportunities in my life…

How I have quietness and peace with God…

Gospel DNA

DNA Marker Five: Self-Sacrifice

Marker Five: Self-Sacrifice
Chapter Twenty-one
The Ultimate Expression of Love

"This is my commandment, that you love one another as I have loved you. Greater love has no one than this, that someone lay down his life for his friends."
Jesus in John 15:12–13

Lilo

"Lilo" is short for Lisolette. I met her after she suffered a stroke and was confined to a wheelchair. Catholic Charities contacted our church in order to seek some help for her. After she had her stroke, the medical staff thought she lost her mind. No one could understand her. She shouted, screamed, cried and acted violently. Nobody could get through to her. Would we pay her a visit?

The invitation was challenging, but I knew we were up to the task. Over the years, the congregation I served demonstrated remarkable love and care for anyone and everyone in need. The followers of Christ in this community of faith were heroes, showing Jesus' love in extraordinary ways. I said "yes" knowing that I could call on an army of servants to reach this precious soul in need.

The first thing we discovered was that Lilo was not crazy. She was frustrated and sad. She was unable to care for herself and her precious dog. She couldn't accomplish daily tasks like she used to, but she wasn't crazy. She just sounded crazy. You see, her stroke caused her to forget the language she learned after she emigrated to the United States: English. Under pressure, she could only remember her childhood language: German. So, when she became frustrated and frightened, she cried out and screamed in German. No one could understand her. For some reason, God led me to study German in high school and college. When I began to dialog with Lilo, I recognized her accent and language. Speaking with her in her native tongue caused her face to brighten and her spirit to become calm. Finally, she was being understood. The floodgates of communication opened and new relationships were ready to begin.

That's when Sandi stepped up to help. Pastoral visits with Lilo could only take place in a limited way. We prayed, visited and shared in Holy Communion, but Lilo needed more than just a once-a-month visit. She needed a friend and advocate. That's why I spoke with Sandi, a woman who lived a life dedicated to caring for people in need. Would she have some time for Lilo? Of course she would. Sandi began to embrace this dear woman in need. Sandi became Lilo's friend. She included Lilo in her life. She visited. She made treats for her. She helped around her apartment—cleaning some very pungent-smelling places and unexpected messes. She aired out the smoke-saturated rooms and allowed her dog get some fresh air. She brought Lilo on outings. After a long time of praying, witnessing, and giving heaping helpings of love and care, Lilo even agreed to be brought to church—her family of faith. I'll never forget the tears in Lilo's eyes and the expression of absolute joy on her face. In Christ, because of Sandi's love, Lilo was a new creation. She was no longer a project on someone's list. She became a loved and cherished human being, a child of God who recognized and embraced the love of Jesus. And, years later, when Lilo became ill and died, we all knew that she was now at home, fully restored, in the presence of her Savior. Love changed a life forever. It took time. It was messy. It was unpredictable. But Sandi would have it no other way. Lilo was worth it.

A Life of Love

Love and self-sacrifice go hand in hand. Self-sacrifice is the flip-side of love. In his sermon, "The Weight of Glory," C.S. Lewis said it well: "If you asked twenty good men to-day what they thought the highest of the virtues, nineteen of them would reply, Unselfishness. But if you asked almost any of the great Christians of old he would have replied, Love..."[122] Lewis points out that the positive characteristic of love is at the heart of self-sacrifice. So, as this book began with love for people, it ends with love for people. It is a love that leads people to make remarkable sacrifices. It is a love that causes people to put their own lives on the line. It is a love that stretches beyond the temporal into the eternal, bringing people to the point of disregarding present sacrifices in order to gain eternal rewards. It is a love fueled by the Holy Spirit and made urgent by the possibility that someone might be lost—separated from God—forever.

The Apostle Paul said to the Christians in Ephesus: "Be imitators of God, therefore, as dearly loved children and live a life of love, just as Christ loved us and gave himself up for us as a fragrant offering and sacrifice to God" (Ephesians 5:1–2 NIV). It is that simple, and it is that serious.

Why does it seem that there is a shortage of love in our nation? True, we love many things. We love sports. We love shopping. We love food. But people? Not so much.

I've already mentioned The Rev. Dr. Berhanu Ofgaa a few times in this book. He commented about the Christian community in Ethiopia: "People are convinced that humanity outside of Christ is lost. The word that is not preferred here [in the U.S.] is 'hell.' Whether we like it or not, the Bible says it. People outside of Christ are doomed to damnation and judgment. Therefore, mission becomes urgent to believers because they don't want others in hell."[123]

When a Gospel movement is happening, people have a sense of urgency about others. They want the best for them—and they want to spare them from the worst. That's why they go to great lengths to reach out to people in their lives.

---

[122] C. S, Lewis, "The Weight of Glory,"
http://www.verber.com/mark/xian/weight-of-glory.pdf, (1942), 1.
[123] Ofgaa, "The Lay Mission Movement in the Ethiopian Evangelical Church Mekane Yesus."

Dr. Ofgaa told the story of a woman who traveled for over twenty miles on a donkey to bring the message of Jesus Christ to a remote village. In the village lived a man who was filled with evil. His presence cast a shadow of darkness and despair over the entire village. He bore resemblance to the demon-possessed man in the fifth chapter of Mark's Gospel. The woman risked her life to bring the Gospel to the man. She was almost killed, but God delivered her from death and changed the heart of the man in the village. When he was brought to faith, the whole village was transformed.

I don't know if we have the same heart for people. Too often the church can seem disconnected and uncaring. Christian communities in the United States can give the impression that they are overwhelmed, busy, self-absorbed and preoccupied. Excitement about sharing the transformational blessing of Jesus seems muted by secular agenda items. We can drift from what God desires His church to be. Henri Nouwen described the worldly tone that can infiltrate the church:

We can take care of ourselves. We do not need God, the Church, or a priest. We are in control. And if we are not, then we have to work harder to get in control. The problem is not lack of faith, but lack of competence. If you are sick, you need a competent doctor; if you are poor, you need competent politicians; if there are technical problems, you need competent engineers; if there are wars, you need competent negotiators. God, the Church, and the minister have been used for centuries to fill the gaps of incompetence, but today, the gaps are being filled in other ways, and we no longer need spiritual answers to practical questions.[124]

Perhaps that is the explanation for today's seeming lack of love and care for people. Perhaps that is why spiritual lethargy has taken hold so strongly in so many circles. We no longer seek spiritual answers. Why is the church shrinking? It must be the birth rate. Perhaps immigration. The church never really cared or

---

[124] Nouwen, *In the Name of Jesus*, 19-20.

reached out; it was simply bloated because of favorable demographic and economic conditions. The Gospel couldn't have been that compelling; it must have been a cultural phenomenon or a sociological response to unique historical conditions. It's impossible to see a Gospel movement in the west similar to what's happening in the global south; the west is too sophisticated.

But evidence throughout the Scriptures and history tells a different story. You've seen that vividly in this book. A new generation reinforces it. There exists today a cadre of people who are tired of selfishness. They are fed up with self-indulgence. They know that spiritual answers are the answers we really need. So they are getting outside of themselves and outside of church walls. They are intent on making not just *a* difference, but *Jesus'* difference in the world. They are forming faith communities, serving the poor, reaching the disenfranchised, eschewing the trappings of the American Dream, and putting their lives on the line to bring the holistic and faithful Gospel to God's precious people. They are living self-sacrificial lives. They are living lives of love. You may know some of these servants of Christ.

It's Simple

A Gospel movement is marked by self-sacrifice. It is saturated with love—Jesus' love. Where can you find this love? How can you instill it in yourself and the people around you? How can you motivate people to live in such a loving way that they will give completely of themselves? You can't. Only the Holy Spirit can impart such love. It's part of what He grows by the grace of God. That is why people put their lives on the line for the Gospel. That is why people give up everything, risk danger, and spend themselves for the sake of God's mission. That is why people can't help but speaking of what they have seen and heard. Because the fruit of the Spirit is love. It is bigger than any of us and any of our plans or efforts. We love only because God first loved us.

A book called *My Church* written for junior high students summed it up well when it explained how the Lutheran Church–Missouri Synod operated. After describing the structure of the denomination, the writer underscored the true heartbeat of the Synod:

> The work which it aims to accomplish is that of preaching the Gospel of Christ. This cannot be done by merely passing resolutions; it can be done only when those who are followers of Christ, individually and collectively, show their love to Him by working for His Kingdom. The work of Synod is the work of all its members. By their contributions, their prayers, [and] their activity in local congregations, the individual Christians are helping, each in his sphere, to carry out the command of Christ: "Preach the Gospel to every creature."[125]

Self-sacrifice happens because we show the love that has been shown to us through the ultimate expression of love—Jesus' sacrifice on the cross for us. That's why we need to ask God for this blessing. We need to pray for this fruit of the Holy Spirit. Before we get to task lists and strategic plans, we need to "draw near to the throne of grace, that we may receive mercy and find grace to help in time of need" (Hebrews 4:16). Drawing near in prayer is a wise starting point.

---

[125] H.O.A. Keinath, *My Church* (St. Louis: Concordia Publishing House, 1947), 136.

Questions for Discussion – Chapter Twenty-one

1. What are your general impressions and thoughts after reading this chapter?

2. What self-sacrifice was involved in the start of your congregation? Share stories if you know them. Research your history to discover the sacrifices if you're not familiar with how your church began.

3. What acts of love helped you to become a follower of Jesus? Recall who made sacrifices for you.

4. How are your story and the story of your church examples of Gospel DNA in action: People, Multiplication, Truth, Adaptability, and Self-sacrifice?

5. Read 2 Corinthians 11:24-29. What sacrifice for the sake of the Gospel is Jesus leading you to make these days?

Gospel DNA Journal:

Why I am grateful for Jesus' sacrifice for me...

How I am being led to grow in living a life of love...

Chapter Twenty-two

Prayer

"Pray also for me, that whenever I open my mouth, words may
be given me so that I will fearlessly make known the mystery of
the gospel, for which I am an ambassador in chains. Pray that I
may declare it fearlessly, as I should."
The Apostle Paul to the Ephesians (6:19–20 NIV)

Pray First

You may remember in Acts chapter 4 when Peter and John
were threatened by the rulers, elders, and scribes in Jerusalem.
After the disciples healed a man who was crippled his whole life,
they were thrown in prison because they were "proclaiming in
Jesus the resurrection from the dead" (Acts 4:2). Five thousand
men believed their message. The church officials were losing
control. They released Peter and John from prison, but threatened
them and told them not to speak or teach in Jesus' name. The
apostles replied, "Whether it is right in the sight of God to listen to
you rather than to God, you must judge, for we cannot but speak of
what we have seen and heard" (Acts 4:19–20). Then they went
back to their fellow believers and reported all that had happened.
What did their friends do? What would we do today? I would
probably try to get some photos of the healing on Facebook. I
would write a nice article with some salient quotes and tweet out
links to it. I might also try to brainstorm a strategy that could share
the principles of what Peter and John did, so their actions could be
replicated over a broader area for greater mission impact. I may
even try to set some numeric goals, perhaps working to double the
number of believers over the next three to six months. Then I
might try to develop a strategy for keeping the opposition out of the
picture.

Those are good goals. They might even be God-pleasing. But Peter and John's fellow believers didn't engage in brainstorming or strategic planning after they heard the report from the apostles. They responded in a different way. They prayed. The immediate reaction of the believers was: "When they heard this, they raised their voices together in prayer to God" (Acts 4:24 NIV). After remembering God the Creator, recognizing the Holy Spirit as the One who spoke through David in the Psalms, and citing the Word of God that foretold the opposition to Jesus, the believers' prayer closed like this:

"And now, Lord, look upon their threats and grant to your servants to continue to speak your word with all boldness, while you stretch out your hand to heal, and signs and wonders are performed through the name of your holy servant Jesus." And when they had prayed, the place in which they were gathered together was shaken, and they were all filled with the Holy Spirit and continued to speak the word of God with boldness (Acts 4:29–31).

Prayer preceded and propelled the movement of the early church. Prayer was first. God was consulted. His answers and directions were awaited. Then steps were taken. Believers surrendered the priority of their will and ideas. They placed themselves in God's hands and moved as His Spirit led them.

It may sound too simple and, perhaps, too easy, but if you want to see the Gospel move in your community and context, the first thing to do is pray—and then keep praying. But you know that prayer is not a simple or easy proposition. In order to pray, we need to put our ambitions and actions on hold. We must wait on God. We need to surrender our bright ideas and slay our egos in order to fall before the Lord of all and ask for His grace and guidance. When we pray, we admit our helplessness and ignorance. Prayer is about self-sacrifice. It is about loving God with all our heart, soul, mind and strength, and seeking Him above ourselves and all others. When we pray, we take the risk that God might change our plans. Our grand schemes and strategies may end up on the cutting room floor. All that is ours may be lost. David Garrison commented about prayer and the movement of the Gospel:

> Prayer permeates Church Planting Movements. Whether it's Koreans rising at four in the morning for a two-hour prayer time, or Spanish Gypsies "going to the mountain," as they call their all night prayer vigils, Church Planting Movements are steeped in prayer. Consequently, prayer has become the first priority of every Church Planting Movement strategist. As soon as a Strategy Coordinator senses the gravity of his calling he immediately falls to his knees and prays, "Oh God, only You can make this happen."[126]

Pray Now

That's why you need to pray right now. If you have any desire to see the Gospel of Jesus Christ turn the heart of anyone you care about to Him, if you want "times of refreshing" to "come from the presence of the Lord" (Acts 3:20) for people you love, for the culture today, and for the world, you need to put this book down for a time and pray. Pray now.

Prayer is first and saturates every moment of a Gospel movement because the Gospel is not ours. It is God's. It is His gift for us and the world. He is the one moving it into people's lives and hearts. We plant and water; God gives growth (1 Corinthians 3:7).

But prayer is something we are tempted to forget about and give up on. Prayer can easily become just a talking point, a conversation item, or a subject for study. Prayer can be pushed aside because we can't control or predict the result. It's not as quantifiable as we would like. Jesus knew this sinful default of ours. That's why He told the parable of the persistent widow:

---

[126] Garrison, *Church Planting Movements*, Kindle Locations 2626-2631.

And he told them a parable to the effect that they ought always to pray and not lose heart. He said, "In a certain city there was a judge who neither feared God nor respected man. And there was a widow in that city who kept coming to him and saying, 'Give me justice against my adversary.' For a while he refused, but afterward he said to himself, 'Though I neither fear God nor respect man, yet because this widow keeps bothering me, I will give her justice, so that she will not beat me down by her continual coming.'" And the Lord said, "Hear what the unrighteous judge says. And will not God give justice to his elect, who cry to him day and night? Will he delay long over them? I tell you, he will give justice to them speedily. Nevertheless, when the Son of Man comes, will he find faith on earth?" (Luke 18:1–8)

As mentioned earlier, Jesus didn't call God's response or faithfulness into question in this parable. He told the story to let His followers know that, if an unrighteous judge answers a pestering widow, won't a loving God respond to His precious people? Of course He will! The big question is: Will we trust God? Will we have faith in who He has revealed Himself to be? Will we tenaciously hold on to His grace and truth when everything looks like it's falling apart? Will we abide in unwavering confidence even when it appears that the Kingdom of God is declining instead of growing? Pray and don't give up, Jesus urged. Only God can make this happen.

I was encouraged as I read the historical literature of my denomination. A prayer priority was clear and bold in its mission focus. Rev. Walter A. Maier, one of God's key driving forces behind the second Gospel movement in the LCMS, wrote an article in the seventy-fifth anniversary book of the LCMS. Maier's comments were about "The Young People in the Missouri Synod." Maier, not yet thirty years old and at the beginning of his ministry, said:

With the statistical records proving that the powerful forces of evil every year succeed in decoying not hundreds, but thousands of our young men and women away from their altars, our Church must be brought to realize more fully that strenuous and organized efforts must be instituted immediately to preserve our youth true to Christ and to secure for themselves a happy and hopeful future. The conviction which forces itself upon all who have lent to the work among the young people even a part of the consideration it truly deserves, is this: We must pray more whole-heartedly and more incessantly for our young people. We must work more zealously and more energetically to counteract the baneful influences so destructive in these days of growing godlessness.[127]

Maier's first inclination was toward prayer. In 1935, Professor Theodore Graebner exhibited the same first-response. In a work called *The Story of Our Church in America*, Graebner commented, "What Can Each Church-Member Do for His Synod? He can pray for it. Let us all remember the missions and colleges of our Synod when we say, 'Hallowed by Thy name; Thy kingdom come!' Has not Jesus given His life for us? Shall we not do all we can to bring others to faith in Him?"[128]

Prayer and self-sacrifice are tied together. Prayer and love walk hand in hand. I cannot emphasize it enough: if you have any desire to see the Gospel move into the lives of your loved ones, into your community, and throughout the world, you need to pray. Practice prayer. Get good at it. Pray constantly. Enlist partners in prayer. Pray as a church, as small groups, as ministry teams, as neighbors, as coworkers, and as a family. Remember those who do not know Jesus. Pray for workers in God's harvest field. Ask God to mercifully bring the gifts of

---

[127] Dau, *Ebenezer*, 439.

[128] Theodore Graebner, *The Story of Our Church in America* (St. Louis: Concordia Publishing House, 1935), 18.

forgiveness and eternal life to those who do not know Him. When you get tired or too busy, redouble your prayer efforts. Humbly fall before your Savior and pray. Ask, seek and knock. Trust in Jesus' promise: "Ask, and it will be given to you; seek, and you will find; knock, and it will be opened to you. For everyone who asks receives, and the one who seeks finds, and to the one who knocks it will be opened" (Matthew 7:7–8).

Hear David Garrison once more:

> We pray because our vision exceeds our abilities. Prayer is the soul's deepest cry of rebellion against the way things are, seeing the lost of this world and crying out, "This does not glorify God, and so, by God's grace, it must change!" Prayer comes from God and ascends back to God on behalf of those who do not know God. Extraordinary prayer lays a firm foundation for a Church Planting Movement.[129]

If you would like to join us in prayer for the mission, you can go to www.txlcms.org/mission-prayer/ for prayer resources and to sign up to be a mission prayer partner. Our hope is that at least 13,200 people begin to pray for a Gospel movement in our context. Let's pray first and pray now. It is part of the DNA marker of self-sacrifice. It is what those who have gone before us lived in radical and astounding ways.

---

[129] Garrison, *Church Planting Movements*, Kindle Locations 2693-2696.

Questions for Discussion – Chapter Twenty-two

1. What prayer thoughts did this chapter give you?

2. How does God's love for us and action for our salvation motivate and shape our prayers?

3. Read Luke 10:1-3. How does Jesus connect prayer with His mission to reach the world?

4. Think about the rhythm of prayer in your life. How can you grow in prayer and how can your prayer life grow in focus on God's mission of salvation for all?

5. Read Psalm 50:15. Prayer is God's gift to us. Why does He treasure our prayers? Call on Him now.

Gospel DNA Journal:

My prayers for the people in my life are...

My prayers for the church and for those who don't know Jesus are...

Marker Five: Self-Sacrifice
Chapter Twenty-three

On the Shoulders of Giants

"Therefore, since we are surrounded by so great a cloud of witnesses, let us also lay aside every weight, and sin which clings so closely, and let us run with endurance the race that is set before us, looking to Jesus, the founder and perfecter of our faith."
Hebrews 12:1–2

Those Who Have Gone Before

Great English physicist, mathematician, astronomer and inventor, Sir Isaac Newton, wrote in a 1675 letter to fellow scientist Robert Hooke, "If I have seen further, it is by standing upon the shoulders of giants."[130] In humility, the thirty-two-year-old Newton understood that if it weren't for the scientists and scholars who came before him, he would not have been able to accomplish his scientific feats.

The same is true of all of us who deeply desire a movement of the Gospel in our time. We stand on the shoulders of giants. In particular, by the grace of God, we stand on the shoulders of the Savior who opened up the way to new life and to life that lasts forever. The Apostle Paul proclaimed, "Let each of you look not only to his own interests, but also to the interests of others. Have this mind among yourselves, which is yours in Christ Jesus, who, though he was in the form of God, did not count equality with God a thing to be grasped, but emptied himself, by taking the form of a servant, being born in the likeness of men. And being found in human form, he humbled himself by becoming

---

[130] "Sir Isaac Newton," http://www.bbc.co.uk/worldservice/learningenglish/movingwords/shortlist/newton.shtml.

obedient to the point of death, even death on a cross" (Philippians 2:4–8). This is Jesus—the Sent One—who sent His disciples: "All authority in heaven and on earth has been given to me. Go therefore and make disciples of all nations, baptizing them in the name of the Father and of the Son and of the Holy Spirit, teaching them to observe all that I have commanded you. And behold, I am with you always, to the end of the age" (Matthew 28:18–20).

By the grace of God, we stand on Jesus' shoulders and the gates of hell cannot prevail against His movement of the Gospel. We also stand on the shoulders of servants of Christ throughout the ages who have sacrificed their wealth, their welfare, and even their lives for the sake of the Gospel.

The people who shared the gospel in the early years of our nation were no lightweights. This was not an easy task. It was a thankless, exhausting, and dangerous undertaking. The efforts of missionaries in the foundational years of the church in our nation—and in my little denomination called the Missouri Synod—were not motivated by programmatic obligations or the quest to become well known. The efforts were made because of the love of Jesus and the sincere desire to reach every person possible with the Good News of life in Him. Christ's love compelled them to urgency and heroic action.

Self-Sacrifice for the Gospel

Pastor Carl Selle is a remarkable example of the Gospel DNA marker of self-sacrifice. He was one of the founding pastors of the Lutheran Church–Missouri Synod in 1847 and the host for the first synodical gathering in Chicago that year. Just eleven years later, he found himself considering a call to serve as pastor in Rock Island, Illinois. By that time, he was serving in Crete, Illinois. As he deliberated about the possible relocation nearly 200 miles to the west and the demands of being pastor for the congregation, teacher for the congregation's school, and missionary for the growing population in this area of the nation, Selle's primary thoughts were not on being comfortable. He did not focus on convenience. His thoughts were on mission. His priority was the movement of the Gospel of Jesus Christ. Selle said:

> It was difficult to take leave of Crete. There I had obviously labored with blessing; there I was intimately joined with many true Christians;...there we had put to rest one of our children on God's acre to slumber waiting for resurrection...But Rock Island seemed to be an important place as a center for mission in the surrounding territory and for areas farther west. Thus I accepted the call but with the condition that school days be limited to three per week and that sufficient time be allowed for mission work.[131]

Leaving the place one of his children was buried and leaving many friends behind, Selle moved to a new place in order to reach new people for Jesus. During his time in Rock Island, he served at least eight additional preaching stations in Illinois and Iowa each month with the help of people from the church. Braving the cold winter winds, long train rides, and primitive meeting places, Selle and his congregation altered the schedule of the school-week and took personal time away from home and family to extend the reach of the Gospel into the growing western frontier.

Selle was also standing on the shoulders of giants. Years earlier, Friedrich Wyneken exhausted himself for the sake of the Gospel. He traveled on horseback and on foot for miles to build relationships with people who needed the Gospel. He was chased off people's land by shotgun-wielding ranchers. Wyneken wrote letters to Germany about his mission work. In one he describes a Sunday filled with preaching, Sunday School, home baptisms and visiting the sick. He was so tired when he finally arrived home late in the evening, he fell immediately into bed for the night. The following Monday he rode thirty-six miles each way to make missionary calls. He spent twelve hours on a horse trying to cover ground that needed many more

---

[131] "Rev. C.A.T. Selle," http://www.angelfire.com/oh5/zionlcms/selle.html.

missionaries. In his letters, he pleaded for help and support.[132] His accounts sound like the stories we hear from Africa today. After Wyneken died in 1876, long before our generation began to write about and laud apostolic gifts among church planters and Gospel movement leaders, C.F.W. Walther remembered Wyneken as "an apostle" of America.

But there was even greater sacrifice. In 1850, J.F. Maier, a twenty-seven-year-old missionary to the Native Americans in Michigan, was traveling with a missionary companion to a remote outreach site. As the two made their way in a small sailboat across Saginaw Bay, they got caught in a terrible storm. The fierce wind and waves broke the vessel's mast. It came crashing down on Pastor Maier, crushing his skull and killing him. Maier's missionary partner drowned as the storm swamped the boat. Their bodies washed up on shore and were discovered by the local Native Americans.[133] These missionaries paid the ultimate price in their effort to share the Good News of Jesus.

Pastor Robert Melhorn made the same sacrifice. He arrived in West Texas in 1894 to help Pastor John Schulenburg of St. Paul Lutheran Church in Fort Worth serve nine mission churches over a 150-mile area. Not long after Melhorn began his mission work, he was caught in a West Texas winter rainstorm as he rode his horse to a church in Wichita Falls.[134] Pastor Melhorn developed pneumonia and never recovered. The young pastor died less that two years after he arrived on the mission field.

Pastor Schulenburg continued the mission work, but was faced with a major decision of his own. He realized that his command of the English language was too poor to bring the people of the growing Fort Worth area the Gospel in the

---

[132] "Mittheilungen aus Briefen des Pastor F. Wyneken in Fort Wayne (N.-Amerika),"http://idb.ub.unituebingen.de/diglit/zlthk_1845/0081/scroll?sid=397 55bdb6f1af18b9ffea55e59efb42f
[133] Zehnder, *Teach My People*, 79.
[134] Koenig, *Pause to Ponder*, 60.

language they spoke. Half of the children in his Sunday School were from unchurched homes. The English language was the way ministry needed to be done. In his heart, he knew he was not the person who could reach the community the way it needed to be reached. So, after thought and prayer, the Rev. John C. Schulenburg resigned his ministry in order to make room for someone who could handle the language of the local population.[135] Imagine the sacrifice!

Texas historian Robert Koenig commented about LCMS mission work in Texas during the late 1800s: "It involved the breaking of paths through areas where roads were non-existent, the fording of unabridged streams at the risk of the missionary's life, the horseback riding in dust storms and rainstorms, the scorching heat of summer and the biting cold of winter."[136]

History tells of servants of Jesus who contracted malaria, suffered exhaustion, discontinued Gospel outreach because of nervous breakdowns, and cobbled together incomes with side jobs in order to feed their families. Why did they endure these hardships? Why did they spend their lives for such suffering? So no one would be lost eternally, but all could rejoice in forgiveness of sins and life everlasting with Jesus.

These are but a few stories of the many sacrifices made by servants of the Gospel to advance the Good News of Jesus. But the stories didn't stop in the 1800s. The intense work and sacrifice continued into the 1900s. One example is Rev. Lorne C. Ruhl. He graduated from Concordia Seminary, St. Louis in 1944 and was sent to Ontario, Canada as a missionary. Ruhl grew up in Ontario, so he ventured back to his childhood region to reach out. His mission field was the northeast border of Ontario and Quebec. Each month he drove 1,000 miles to serve seven mission churches in the area. When the heavy snow came in the winter, he used both train and bus to reach the scattered mission communities. He left on Saturday, did all he could to extend the Gospel at his mission stations, and returned on

---

[135] Koenig, *Pause to Ponder*, 117.
[136] Koenig, *Pause to Ponder*, 61.

Wednesday. But there was still more work to be done. Ruhl addressed the Ontario District Convention in 1945 and spoke about the "new Ontario mission frontier." He urged delegates to send more missionaries into the mission field because much more could be accomplished in these remote places where so many still needed to hear the Good News of Jesus. During his ninety-seven years of life, Rev. Ruhl was instrumental in starting ten new churches.[137]

Spiritual Heroes

These people did not set out to become heroes. They weren't looking for accolades or attention. They were simply taking seriously the injunction of Christ to "Go!". With fear and trembling and great devotion they were serving as stewards of the mysteries of God. They couldn't bear the thought of one person being separated from Christ for eternity. They knew the healing and consoling power of the forgiveness of sins. They yearned for every person to understand the blessing of Jesus' presence and peace.

We need spiritual heroes today. The methods may be different. The ministries may be unique. The contexts may have changed. But there is no substitute for bold and self-sacrificial love in the name of Jesus. God opens remarkable and surprising doors of opportunity to serve Him and to reach His beloved people. The DNA of self-sacrifice from our self-sacrificial Savior is embedded in the lives of His redeemed. We need to reconnect with this beautiful DNA.

Fortunately, God is raising up many who are.

---

[137] Michael Ruhl, "The LCMS Church Planting Journey" (paper written about his father, 2015).

Questions for Discussion – Chapter Twenty-three

1. What thoughts and insights did you have as you read the stories of sacrifice in this chapter?

2. How does the beautiful message of forgiveness and new life by God's grace through faith in Jesus fill you with passion and excitement to share this Good News with others—even in the face of sacrifice?

3. What urgency exists in sharing the Gospel with others?

4. Read Revelation 1:4-9. What self-sacrifice do you see in these verses? How does this self-sacrificial love impact your life?

5. What sacrifices does speaking the truth call for in our day and age?

Gospel DNA Journal:

I am thankful for the ways God has sacrificed for me...

How God cultivates selflessness in me...

Marker Five: Self-Sacrifice
Chapter Twenty-four
Sacrifice Grows

"In the world you will have tribulation. But take heart; I have
overcome the world."
Jesus in John 16:33

Hope for the Future

The ministry in which I serve gives me great hope. As one who helps facilitate mission work in Texas, I get to see and meet people who have been moved by the Holy Spirit to give time, talent, and treasure for the sake of the Gospel. In addition to having the privilege of walking with missionaries in Texas, it is heartening to meet self-sacrificial Gospel servants from around the nation who are embracing Gospel DNA by the grace of God.

David Garrison noted that self-sacrifice is a consistent characteristic of movements of the Gospel—many times, extreme self-sacrifice. He said, "As the Church Planting Movement panel discussed the various Church Planting Movements we had witnessed, one unavoidable factor surfaced again and again. So many of the missionary colleagues we had known, who were instrumental in these Church Planting Movements, were no longer serving as missionaries. Others have continued on the mission field, but only after enduring staggering calamities."[138]

The outward hardships are only half the story. Every Gospel servant becomes engaged in a fierce spiritual battle. As the Apostle Paul declared: "Finally, be strong in the Lord and in the strength of his might. Put on the whole armor of God, that you may be able to stand against the schemes of the devil. For

---

[138] Garrison, *Church Planting Movements*, Kindle Locations 3797-3800.

we do not wrestle against flesh and blood, but against the rulers, against the authorities, against the cosmic powers over this present darkness, against the spiritual forces of evil in the heavenly places" (Ephesians 6:10–12). The devil seeks to make war "on those who keep the commandments of God and hold to the testimony of Jesus" (Revelation 12:17). But the crucified and risen Christ has thrown Satan down. The testimony of Jesus repels the evil one (Revelation 12:10-11). We are fully aware of the devil's strategies (2 Corinthians 2:11). And we are no ordinary people. Redeemed by the blood of Jesus Christ, everything has changed. The Apostle Peter informed us of our new identity: "But you are a chosen race, a royal priesthood, a holy nation, a people for his own possession, that you may proclaim the excellencies of him who called you out of darkness into his marvelous light" (1 Peter 2:9). We are given all we need to follow in the steps of Jesus and to shine His light in the darkness of the world. So many have heard that call.

Self-Sacrifice Today

One such group is a faith community of new immigrants from the Middle East who fled their countries due to religious persecution. These believers in Christ have lost their homes, jobs, bank accounts and contact with extended family members for the sake of their Savior. Now they are reaching out into the local community to bring faith in Jesus to fellow immigrants. They worship in the Arabic language. Their pastor is a professor of Arabic at a university one-hundred miles away. He commutes every Sunday to lead worship and, at times, stays with the congregation for the whole weekend to serve church members, train new disciples, and reach out to the community with the Gospel.

A young woman who was recently baptized by this pastor commented about her new walk of faith: "I was born and raised in a Muslim family…The stories about Jesus were brought to us as myths and legends, thus not true. As time passed, I started to realize that I was [on] a wrong path." Then one of the men from the congregation began to share Jesus with her as they commuted to work together. She said, "[He] talked to me a lot about Jesus and how graceful and merciful He is. He showed me many movies about Jesus and stories of miracles performed by Jesus. I started to realize [how] loving Jesus is and how much He cares about me. He has always been with me at my bad and good times." Because of the sacrifice of many, this Russian Muslim woman now confesses the name of Jesus and shines His light to people around her.

In many ways, new arrivals to the United States are leading the way in the movement of the Gospel. In our nation where complacency and self-satisfaction have commanded the lives of many, a perspective of gratitude, sacrifice, and Gospel urgency arrives with immigrants who have experienced deprivation and struggle we do not know as intimately on our shores. I work with a man who came from Africa as a refugee. He was persecuted by an oppressive regime, fought and was wounded in a civil war, fled to another nation, was separated from his family, began work as an evangelist under a missionary to the region, and rescued his loved ones from tribal threats of death. He endured long separation from the woman he loved, learned new languages—including English—and became a pastor. This man's faith and life formation is far removed from the context of a safe and insulated life in suburbia. He brings with him passion and perspective for Gospel outreach. He understands human brokenness and the desperate need for God, our refuge, strength and Savior.

Another missionary with whom I am privileged to serve came to America with the DNA of a Gospel movement planted firmly in his life. He grew up in a church planter's home. His father started a church in their living room and proceeded to plant eighteen additional faith communities. Week after week my missionary colleague and his father traveled by mule to each of these new congregations. The experience shaped in this man a missionary heart. He soon entered training to become a pastor in his home country, but after he completed his schooling, the government closed all the churches, confiscated church properties, and imprisoned and tortured pastors and evangelists. Even this man was imprisoned for six months. After his release from prison, he fled the area and served in a variety of ministries. He continued to plant churches and, with his wife, founded an agency that helps orphans in his home country. Today, he is in the United States with a vision to plant churches among immigrants from his nation and the surrounding community. God has "imported" an infusion of active Gospel DNA to help catalyze a movement of the Gospel in the United States.

Dozens of pastors and laypeople in our nation are serving in ministry while they work in the marketplace. Many work long hours to support their families, take coursework for ministry formation, and spearhead new mission development with virtually every spare moment. Some of these self-sacrificial servants have left homes, relatives and familiar surroundings. They endure the disheartening challenges of apathy toward, and rejection of, the Gospel. They hail from nations abroad and communities across the U.S. Some have young children to care for. Others are putting kids through college. At times, their spouses support their ministries by working long hours to make ends meet. These are the spiritual heroes of our time. Some go to places others have no desire to go. They hold the hands of the homeless, walk with addicts, befriend the unwanted, travel long hours to serve people in remote and forgotten places, and cross the barriers of race and ethnicity to build bridges of Christ's love. These servants are not driven by self-interest. They are not searching for riches or renown. They know that the most important gift in life is the gift of Jesus Christ and the new life He gives. They love people as Christ loves people.

A woman who is reaching out to her female Muslim friends took my hand recently, looked me in the eyes and said, "Please pray for us. The task is so hard. Sometimes I think I am losing, but we keep opening the Bible and talking about Jesus. Please pray." The Gospel DNA of self-sacrifice is alive and well. We do need to pray. We need to support and encourage one another as partners in mission. We need to ask the Savior to bring to completion the wonderful work He has started. We need the Good News of life in Jesus to sweep across our land.

Words of Love

How do we move forward? Words from the past bring encouragement and direction. Listen to the tone set by a 1943 publication called *The Approach to the Unchurched*. They are words for us today:

> The world is extremely worldly. The social order is extremely irreligious. The economic order is extremely unstable. The nations are extremely hateful and revengeful. The hope for a better world lies in the possibility of the rule of Christ in the hearts of sinners. It is the divine duty and the great privilege of every Christian to bring the Christless the message of true peace and everlasting salvation...Christian service offers no more exalted possibility than that of being instrumental in winning a person from a life of sin to a life in Christ.[139]

> It is the story of the soul winner of today. He is most successful in the work of the individual for the individual. Nothing can ever substitute for close personal contact of life with life. We shall do well to imitate the example of our Lord and His disciples in the use of this method of individual appeal.[140]

The author, Pastor Philip Lange, goes on to say, "It's going to cost something if we set out in earnest to approach and evangelize souls. Very often time, energy, comfort, popularity, social standing, and many other things, must be sacrificed."[141]

---

[139] Lange, *The Approach*, 3.

[140] Lange, *The Approach*, 7.

[141] Lange, *The Approach*, 21.

These are words of love for people. They call us to take time with people, to show real care, and to bring noble answers to the confounding questions we face in our day. They call for a reconnection with the DNA marker of self-sacrifice. At the 1950 LCMS convention, President J.W. Behnken said, "We must train our people ever better to do personal mission work."[142] Later in that convention a resolution was adopted with the bold statement: "Resolved, That the Lutheran Church–Missouri Synod call upon its total membership for an even greater love and devotion to the Lord and Savior of mankind, and a consequent burning zeal for the lost souls of men."[143]

Resolutions can't change hearts, but the love of Christ can and does. His love ignites in us a love for people. His sacrifice for us moves us to sacrifice for one another. How can we take steps forward to become reconnected with Gospel DNA and to see a Gospel movement take hold among us?

---

[142] *Proceedings of the Forty-first Regular Convention of the Lutheran Church–Missouri Synod* (St. Louis: Concordia Publishing House, 1950), 5.
[143] *Proceedings*, 426.

Questions for Discussion – Chapter Twenty-four

1. What new thoughts did you have as you read this chapter?

2. What evidence do you see of the spiritual battle involved with the movement of the Gospel?

3. Read 1 Peter 2:9. Talk about how these verses encourage you as you see your new identity in Christ and how they help you serve as God's instrument for bringing Jesus' love to others.

4. What stories of missionaries inspired you? What new thoughts did the stories stir up in you about outreach with the Gospel in your context?

5. You read the quote: "Nothing can ever substitute for close personal contact of life with life." Why are personal relationships so important for sharing the Good News of Jesus? What self-sacrifice might be involved in cultivating authentic personal relationships with others?

Gospel DNA Journal:

Personal relationships I am being led to cultivate as a follower of Christ...

What I am willing to sacrifice to share my faith...

Marker Five: Self-Sacrifice
Chapter Twenty-five
How to Activate Gospel DNA

"If anyone would come after me, let him deny himself and take
up his cross daily and follow me."
Jesus to His followers in Luke 9:23

The Way Forward

What are the next steps for the church? How can followers of Jesus move forward with Gospel DNA? The diagnosis and the path forward were charted out well by Missouri Synod assistant to the president Lawrence Meyer:

Today, in the hearts of too many [people] of our Church, the phrase "men are lost" seems to call forth no spiritual emotion whatsoever. But listen to what Jesus says in the 15th chapter of Luke. Indeed, like a lost coin men are useless; like a lost sheep they are helpless; like the lost boy they are unspeakably hopeless.

The reason why most churches of the past have lost the heritage of the Gospel is that they no longer cared for, no longer gave away, no longer reflected, the true Light of the world to the world. The Gospel of Jesus Christ can change the lives and hearts of men. But where are the [believers] of conviction who will declare it to the world?

The history of church organizations has usually been as follows: A church organization has a lowly beginning. Then it gathers impetus, and as it increases in momentum, it begins to increase until it becomes a large body. It grows rich. It becomes satisfied with itself. It grows lax, then worldly.

Finally it ceases to evangelize. Instead of increasing, it begins to decline, and in the end the members begin to wonder why, although they have not openly denied the faith, they nevertheless come under the condemnation of Him who said to the church at Laodicea, "I know thy works that thou art neither hot or cold."

Christ is the true Light of the world. If we are to follow His injunction to be the light of the world, then we must repent, and follow Him, and learn, and pray, and serve.

There is no easy road forward. God's way forward is always hard. It was thus for His Son, and it will be for us. The call to be the light of the world comes not from Synod or from any individual in Synod, but from God Himself. He calls the members of the Church today to dispel the gross darkness in the turmoil and confusion of the world by carrying forward His Gospel to all the world, holding aloft Him who is the Light of the world—Jesus Christ, and Him crucified.[144]

If we lose the passion for people who do not know Jesus, if we cease to evangelize because we are self-satisfied or fearful, if we have forgotten our heritage and no longer give away the true Light of the world to the world, then, as Meyer said so eloquently and passionately, "we must repent, and follow Him, and learn, and pray, and serve." What might this look like in the framework of Gospel DNA markers?

People

In her article called "The Loneliness of American Society," Janice Shaw Crouse reported that a recent study by sociologists at Duke and the University of Arizona found that one in four people "have no one with whom they can talk about their personal troubles or triumphs." If family members were removed from the equation, the number of Americans who have no one to

---

[144] Meyer, *Torch Bearers*, 14, 59, 63-64.

talk to about important things in life more than doubles. The isolation, Crouse notes, is driven by many factors. The cultural push for personal freedom, the breakdown of the family, the increased draw of television and media, and longer commute times all contribute, as Rabbi Daniel Lapin says, to "raising a generation of children who are orphans in time…They wander aimlessly about without connections—physically, emotionally, or spiritually." Crouse then ties together the many strands of cultural and social developments with a spiritual commentary:

> Finally, the secular humanist view that human existence is disconnected from any higher power and from responsibility for anyone other than ourselves gives a certain freedom to make one's own rules, but there is a price to pay for this freedom. Gone is human dignity. Gone is mankind's special connection to the Author of beauty, truth, or goodness. Ultimately, we are "free," but autonomy is just another way of being alone. Autonomous individuals have no responsibility to others, just as others have no claim on them. There is no obligation to care about others' troubles, or even to listen when someone intrudes into another's priceless personal space in search of a sympathetic hearing of their concerns and difficulties.[145]

We need to ask ourselves, have we, as the church, as followers of Jesus, absorbed the secular humanist point of view about human existence so completely, that our drive for personal autonomy is overriding God's calling to care about people? Do we focus on ourselves so much that we have very little concern for people's eternal welfare? Is personal satisfaction so dominant in our lives that zeal for the message of God's love in Jesus Christ fades and falls from importance? Are we simply blending in with the secular world when "the phrase 'men are lost' seems to call forth no spiritual emotion whatsoever"?

---

[145] Janet Shaw Crouse, "The Loneliness of American Society," The *American Spectator*, May 18, 2014, http://spectator.org/articles/59230/loneliness-american-society.

But we have a higher a calling. It is the noble, holy and worthy pursuit of Jesus who came to seek and to save the lost (Luke 19:10). It is the joyful course of bringing Good News to the poor and freedom to those who are oppressed (Luke 4:18). It is, as the Apostle Paul said, a way that exceeds all other pathways and focal points in life (1 Corinthians 12:31). We have been given the opportunity to love others as God has loved us.

By God's grace, fed and nurtured with His Word of truth, infused with His courage and boldness, can we, as followers of Christ, create a new narrative in our culture—and in the church? Can our voices cultivate love for people even as other loud voices around us insist on selfishness, divisiveness, annoyance and hatred? Can we bring the blessing of the Gospel of peace, the joy of the forgiveness of sins, and the certainty of eternal life to an uncertain and turbulent world? Reaching outside the walls of the church, in relationship with others, with excitement about the gift of new life in Jesus Christ, can we show sincere love to all people by actively "holding aloft Him who is the Light of the world—Jesus Christ, and Him crucified"?

Multiplication

While preparing to speak at the 90th anniversary of a congregation in San Antonio, I reviewed the history of LCMS church development there. It was saturated with Gospel DNA. A new church was started, on average, every three years—ten churches from the mid-1920s to the mid-1950s as the city doubled in size from about 200,000 to over 400,000 people. Three of the churches began as preaching stations—efforts of local congregations to reach new communities with the Gospel. Five of the churches started as a result of neighborhood mission canvasses and the calling of missionaries. One congregation was started as a "defense mission"—a church that served people displaced by the war effort in the early 1940s. Another new mission began as an experiment of the Lutheran Men's Clubs in San Antonio. They canvassed a neighborhood, started a congregation, engaged the help of a local vicar, and called a pastor as the outreach grew into a larger congregation.[146]

Efforts to multiply God's Kingdom were the norm. Followers of Christ, congregations, and church workers eagerly searched for people who needed the Gospel. The multiplication of new believers, new congregations, and new servant-leaders is what people expected during that era. Displaced people were not ignored. New neighborhoods were explored. People tried new things to reach new people with the Good News of Jesus Christ. It took work, but it was joyful labor. It meant expending resources, but the results yielded true riches. Gospel DNA was evident and active.

Can multiplication become normal again? Can the Gospel movements seen in our history teach us to do again what we did at first (Revelation 2:5)? In simple and enterprising ways, with joy, can we do new things to reach new people with the blessing of new life in Jesus Christ?

Truth

It became evident during the research process for this book that two factors contributed to pauses in Gospel movements in the United States. These factors were mentioned by Lawrence Meyer in his statements at the beginning of this chapter. First, Meyer said, the church "grows lax, then worldly." Part of being lax and worldly is drifting from, or intentionally surrendering, the truth of the Scriptures. Too many vibrant Gospel outreach efforts of Christian churches stalled when the message of Jesus Christ crucified and risen, the call to faith in Him, and the Word of God as the source and norm of faith and life became secondary or optional components of increasingly secular church organizations. Without the truth, the church became a social organization with no power or promise. The Gospel faded from prominence and caused the church to decline. True doctrine, sound Scriptural teaching—the Gospel message—is the heart and center of Gospel DNA.

---

[146] Koenig, *Pause to Ponder*, 135-136, 257-260.

Meyer added another reason for the decline of the church. He said, "[The church] ceases to evangelize." While some denominations jettisoned the truth, other church organizations turned inward with the truth. They grew distracted by church business or conflict. They became fearful about cultural changes. Institutional complexity interfered with organic outreach. Preferences and prejudice alienated outsiders. The love of Christ was no longer the primary compelling stimulus of the church, so the movement of the Gospel was placed on pause.

God has a much better plan for His Church. He knits truth and love together. Can we relearn the art of both preserving AND promoting the truth of the Gospel? By God's grace, can we refrain from separating truth and mission? Can we be retaught to see the whole truth as both sound teaching and active evangelization? As redeemed children of God, can we make the commitment to speak the truth in love? This is the DNA that leads to Gospel movements.

Adaptability

Adaptability does not mean compromising doctrine. Being adaptable is not about focusing on changes in worship style. The heart of adaptability is, as Lawrence Meyer emphasized, "[Dispelling] the gross darkness in the turmoil and confusion of the world by carrying forward [Christ's] Gospel to all the world." Adaptability asks, "How can we accomplish the urgent calling of bringing salvation in Jesus Christ to all people?" Adaptability is innovative movement of the Gospel founded on unwavering faithfulness to the Gospel. Essentially, being adaptable means following in God's footsteps and doing exactly what He did time and time again: He assessed new situations and acted accordingly for the salvation of His people.

Is it possible for us not only to accept change but to expect change? Can we willingly and joyfully plan on changing methods to bring an unchanging Christ to a changing world? What if we proactively followed the Apostle Paul's pattern of life and ministry expressed in his statement: "For though I am free from all, I have made myself a servant to all, that I might win more of them" (1 Corinthians 9:19)? A Gospel movement depends on the DNA marker of adaptability.

Self-Sacrifice

Self-sacrifice begins with Jesus. The Apostle John said it very clearly: "This is how we know what love is: Jesus Christ laid down his life for us" (1 John 3:16). What words can describe God's incredible love? He sent His beloved Son to live a sinless life in our stead, to be put to death for our sin and guilt, to conquer death through His resurrection, and to ascend into heaven with the promise of His triumphant return. We were lost, but Jesus came to seek and to save us. Now we are never alone. Now we have eternal hope. What mercy! What grace! What complete self-sacrifice!

John continued his thought in verse 16: "And we ought to lay down our lives for our brothers." God's gracious self-sacrifice in Jesus Christ begets self-sacrifice. We love because God first loved us (1 John 4:19). We live with the sacred obligation to put our lives out there for other people so they, too, know the love of God. This is the joyful privilege of making Jesus known. This is God's mandate to use our time, our money, and our talents for the sake of the Gospel. This is Christ's commission to go and share His gifts in spite of our doubts and fears. This is Jesus' bidding to surrender our preferences, our comfort zones, and our routines in order to bring the gift of new life in Him to the world. Jesus said, "If anyone would come after me, let him deny himself and take up his cross and follow me. For whoever would save his life will lose it, but whoever loses his life for my sake and the gospel's will save it" (Mark 8:34–35).

Can there be any better gift to give? Is any message more hope-filling or more life-restoring? After Jesus told the parables of the lost sheep and the lost coin in Luke chapter 15, he described the great gain and the unspeakable joy of this calling to self-sacrificial love. He said, "I tell you, there will be more joy in heaven over one sinner who repents than over ninety-nine righteous persons who need no repentance" (Luke 15:7). The Savior who welcomed sinners and ate with them made it very clear that this is what God and His people do. They scour the countryside for the lost sheep. They turn the house upside down for the lost coin. They have an unstoppable zeal for bringing God's rescue to all people. It is their purpose and priority.

What is the result of this self-sacrifice? A movement of the Gospel. Activated by the grace of God through faith in Him, Gospel DNA will flow like streams in the desert. People like Whitney will receive the blessing of Jesus' love and salvation from followers of Christ who care deeply about the eternal welfare of others. People like Whitney will share this life-changing truth with others. Followers of Christ will multiply. In their own contexts, they will go to sacrificial lengths to bring the gift they have been given to others. As it has for thousands of years, the Gospel will continue to move. New people will come to faith. New churches will start. New servant-leaders will be raised up.

Shall we go there? The way is not hidden or complicated. It is not an elusive goal or foolish pipedream. God is doing this around the world. And He has done this among us. Shall we give our attention to the life-giving markers of Gospel DNA in order to see a flourishing church initiate a simple, beautiful, and sweeping movement of the Gospel in and through the lives of God's precious people?

Let us heed the wise words of the prophet once again: "Listen to me, you who pursue righteousness, you who seek the Lord: look to the rock from which you were hewn, and to the quarry from which you were dug" (Isaiah 51:1). Gospel DNA is alive and well. It is normal for the body of Christ to engage in Gospel movement thinking and action. Let us look to the Rock from which we were hewn. Let us look to Jesus Christ to see who we really are and ask Him to bring us along in a new movement of the Gospel.

Questions for Discussion – Chapter Twenty-five

1. After examining Gospel DNA in this book, what new thoughts and directions do you have about the church and about your life as a follower of Christ?

2. Read Luke 15:1-7. What bold Gospel DNA do you detect in Jesus' parable?

3. What insights and thoughts have you gained as you've examined the five markers of Gospel DNA:
   a. People
   b. Multiplication
   c. Truth
   d. Adaptability
   e. Self-Sacrifice

4. At the beginning of this chapter, Lawrence Meyer assessed how the church declines and what pathway is needed for the church to move forward. Now that you have finished reading this book, what must the church guard against as it faces the future?

5. What does the church need to cultivate as it moves into the future? Apply your answers to your church and your life.

Gospel DNA Journal:
Next steps for me and for my church…

How God's promises give me confidence about the future…

Acknowledgments

My sincere gratitude goes to all who have assisted with this project and to all who have encouraged and taught me during the development of this material: To Ken, Steve, Jon, Yohannes, John, Paul and Lou—colleagues in mission; To Jeff and Jon, and all the pioneers in mission from the Lutheran Society For Missiology (http://www.lsfm.global); To Mark and the ministry of the Concordia Historical institute; To Ben and for all the resources and excitement he brought from the library at Concordia Seminary in St. Louis; To Dr. Eugene Krentz for his first-hand input regarding the history of the LCMS and his reviewing expertise; To Hannah for her timely, cheerful and expert copy-editing; To all the people who have listened to my presentations and offered wise advice, material and stories; To the missionaries who serve heroically on the front lines and to those who have gone before; To Bryant for his encouragement to stretch beyond the conventional; To Cindy who gives up so much so I can devote time to writing and who loves me unconditionally; and to Jesus for His love, His mission, and for giving me the privilege of serving Him and His people.

About the Author

Michael Newman has served in ministry since 1987. Married to his wife Cindy since 1983, they have been blessed with two wonderful daughters and the most beautiful granddaughter in the world. When not preaching, teaching, or writing, you might catch him hanging out with his family, running a few miles on the Texas roads, or enjoying a good book.

More books written by Michael W. Newman:
The Life You Crave: It's All About Grace
Struggle Well
Satan's Lies
Revelation: What the Last Book of the Bible Really Means
What Happens When You Die
There is No God. Or is There?
Steps forward
Harrison Town
To find more resources and information, go to **www.mnewman.org.**

Made in the USA
Middletown, DE
16 May 2016